DATE DUE

SEXUAL ETHICS
AND CHRISTIAN RESPONSIBILITY

SEXUAL

AND

RESPONSIBILITY

Edited by

NEW YORK

ETHICS
CHRISTIAN
SOME DIVERGENT VIEWS

JOHN CHARLES WYNN

ASSOCIATION PRESS

Also edited by
John Charles Wynn
SEX, FAMILY, AND SOCIETY IN
THEOLOGICAL FOCUS

Foreword

Although their views *are* divergent, the authors in this symposium do converge on a common objective: they seek a path consistent with Christian ethics in a search through what Vance Packard has dubbed our sexual wilderness.

This symposium is the sequel to *Sex, Family and Society in Theological Focus* (Association Press, 1966); and, like that volume, is designed either for group study or personal reading. The earlier series was a preparatory volume for The Second North American Conference on Church and Society held at McMaster University in May, 1966. This volume follows as an attempt to probe further some of the refractory questions that conference raised. It is published as a contribution to the current debate raging over sexual behavior, and is dedicated by the editor to

> The Reverend Edward Payson Linnell
> Father—in-faith;
> Father—in-law.
> JOHN CHARLES WYNN, EDITOR

Contents

SEXUAL ETHICS
AND CHRISTIAN RESPONSIBILITY

1

Confounded Theologians

•

JOHN CHARLES WYNN

In his introductory essay the editor contends that although "sexual revolution" is a useless term, the sexual behavior of our day is forcing theologians to rethink their doctrine. John Charles Wynn is professor of church education in an ecumenical consortium, The Rochester Center for Theological Studies. His previous writings include *Pastoral Ministry To Families, How Christian Parents Face Problems,* and with co-author Roy W. Fairchild, *Families In The Church: A Protestant Survey.* In addition he has edited *Sermons On Marriage and Family Life* and *Sex, Family and Society In Theological Focus.*

•

THEOLOGIANS TODAY ARE CONFOUNDED by the awe-ful challenge to derive guidance for contemporary problems in sexual behavior from the historic Christian tradition. Laws and regulations of past centuries can appear irrelevant to contemporary sexual problems. And many of the sexual questions of our day are hardly mentioned in biblical doctrine. Teachings of Jesus offer no specific reference to some of the questions that are most difficult in this era. We can cite no sayings from him about premarital coition, petting to orgasm, homosexuality, abortion, contraception, or artificial insemination. At a time when the church is under attack from left and right, when the new breed of clergymen are testing old ecclesiastical directions, when the new theology is stretching old canons, we find the new morality calling both absolute rules and the old natural law into account.

A search through eleven recently published books by Christian writers, for example, reveals that ten of the eleven allow for some unusual situation in which non-marital intercourse might be justifiable. Such a finding could not have been possible a generation ago. Now, however, the justification for non-marital sexual contacts in unusual circumstances is presented not only in theory as in *Honest Sex* by Rustum and Della Roy, but also through concrete case histories in the books of Joseph Fletcher, James Pike, and Hans Hofmann. Tom Driver has written that the church fears sex; and he is doubtless correct. But the church appears to fear grappling with the problem of sex less and less as the world about shows less inhibitions concerning the issue.

Some two decades ago we began to use the label, "sex revolution," to describe the startling alterations in the attitudes and behavior of male and female in our society. Yet the label was inexact for the phenomenon. A revolution is a fundamental change in direction, technically a complete turn-around. What has happened in sexual behavior is nothing of that sort, but a continuation in the same direction—and at accelerated speed. It can be said that the Copernican Revolution completely altered man's way of looking at his universe. It can even be argued that the American Revolution produced a similarly radical change in man's political philosophy. The trends in sexual behavior, by such comparison, look peculiarly unrevolutionary. They might more appropriately bear Vance Packard's title of sexual wilderness or perhaps Ira Reiss's sexual renaissance.

Meanwhile the influence of the church upon people's conduct has been measurably decreasing. Gallup Poll statistics mark an annual decline in the number of respondents who feel that their church is maintaining any notable effect upon persons. Rodney Stark and Charles Y. Glock corroborate the Gallup finding in their book, *American Piety: The Nature of Religious Commitment,* citing from their survey that both orthodox religious belief and obedience to a rule-centered morality have been lessening among church members throughout the past decade.

YOUTH CONFOUNDS THE ELDERS

In the midst of its multiple challenges, the church is beginning to work through new understandings of Christian ethics and of sexual morality. This book is but one evidence of that effort.

The World Council of Churches, for instance, was again forced to face up to the issue of sexual morality at the massive assembly at Uppsala in 1968. The delegates were confronted, among the numerous documents that fomented discomfort, with one that questioned whether modern methods of preventing conception will usher in a new era when sleeping together may become as ordinary as eating together. The paper went on to remind delegates that chastity is more than abstinence from copulating. Too often chastity is considered purely in terms of abstinence and keeping intercourse within marriage. But "Chastity," the papers argues, "is surely also concerned with the way love is expressed, with the qualities of tenderness and responsibility which not only restrain

people in their personal relations but also sustain husband and
wife in a life-long commitment to each other." Radical in its theology, the statement continued, "We believe that physical intercourse, personal commitment and marriage form a dynamic
unity . . . Legalism and judgment upon others are not ways of
living up to this."

Indeed churchmen now defend less vigorously the absolute rules
and legalism meant to be common moral standards applicable to
all. Rules of living, many Christians believe, must relate to real
situations; who the person is, the nature of his calling and commitment, and where and under what circumstances he lives. Person
and community are inseparable. Personal responsibility can be
solved only within the framework of community. Persons differ
widely and must be respected as individuals, God's children. We
dare not reduce their style of living to mere rules lest we become
blind to the signs of the times through which God is speaking to
us.

Yet such rule-centered morality is the predominant standard
that adult churchmen have attempted to press upon young people,
although without notable success. Young people the world over
are rebelling and are experimenting with new styles of living. Some
are acting out as hippies; some are staging rebellions in universities; some are opposing the police. It is small wonder that they also
rebel against the official code of sexual morality elders have pressed
upon them. Many young people have begun to challenge any authority which is not authentically earned. Respect only for the
sake of age is not cogent to them. In the Western world they live
in a society that has extended their childhood an additional ten
years beyond the onset of physical adolescence, retarding them
from adult prerogatives and mature responsible freedom. To understand these facts is to comprehend better the context for some
recent sexual behavior of youths, both within and outside the
church.

THE NEW MORALITY

Confronted by this material, delegates to the World Council's assembly were compelled to consider the impact of the new morality. In this they were hardly alone. For the new morality, a term first attributed to Pius XII, of all people, covers a variety of ethical theories that touch on nearly everyone: situationism, contextualism, existentialism, relativism, and the new casuistry.

The new morality is committed to freedom; and therein lies its risk. Paul Lehmann, in his *Ethics In A Christian Context*, notes that the sexual act is as open as any other action to freedom in obedience to God. For him, Christian ethics offers

> a context within which sexual intensity can be creatively related to sexual sensitivity because sexuality itself has been transformed from a biological to a human fact, from an elemental drive which man has in common with animals to a distinctively human relation inwardly shaped and guided by what is specifically human in human nature and by what gives fundamental meaning to human life. (p. 138)

This same concern for what it means to be a genuinely free human being in the creation of God informs the writing of Joseph Fletcher (*Situation Ethics: The New Morality*). For him "love's decisions are made situationally, not prescriptively" (p. 134) with "the situationist cutting himself loose from the dead hand of unyielding law." (p. 135) Fletcher then sets forth several situations in the Appendix of his book that describe how the sexual choice is made within the new morality. Most memorable among these is the case of Mrs. Bergmaier, imprisoned in a European concentration camp, who achieves her release and return to family by becoming pregnant with the aid of a guard.

The Reformation impressed Protestant Christianity with a categorical doctrine, re-emphasized by Martin Luther, that we are justified by grace alone in our faith. This central reformed doctrine puts law and regulation in a new light. Churchmen have not always known how to interpret this theological insight, nor yet the new morality (for his time) of St. Paul who assures the Galatians:

"You are not under the law." (5:18) Untrusting of human choice, both theologian and man-in-the-pew have grudgingly allowed that the Christian might be free from the law's burden in some acts; but almost never in his sexual conduct.

THEOLOGICAL INSIGHTS FOR ETHICS

Theology, we are assured, must inform any system of ethics. We derive our ethical propositions from our knowledge of God. According to an ancient formula (Micah 6:8) we shall ask, What does the *Lord* require of you? Thus we are obligated to identify those theological foundations that aid us in discerning the points of human experience through which God can speak to our time.

This concept of God speaking to us (a necessarily anthropomorphic figure of speech) is faithfully biblical. The God revealed in the Old Testament was sometimes dubbed "the God who speaks." And how is he understood to speak? Chiefly through persons and their relationships his word is revealed to us. Through his prophets he has made himself known, and then climactically through his Son (Heb. 1:1).

God also speaks through history. This fundamental conviction of the Judaeo-Christian tradition means not only that God has made his disclosures through the events of biblical times, e.g. the travail of Israel or the beginnings of the church, but also in the events of contemporary history. Could it be that even in the development of progesterone which makes possible the oral contraceptive, or could it be that through the erotic stimulation of our sex-saturated society we can discern his meaning in our own history?

Moreover it is especially fitting to note that theological insights frequently come out of turmoil and times of dissonance. Because we are presented with problems, we then begin to think about them theologically. The popular picture of a saintly, tranquil thinker formulating theological propositions in a secluded ivory tower is, for the most part, a canard. Theological understanding has more often come out of polemic, pressure and turmoil. Thus *The City of God* was written by Augustine when his Roman civilization was crumbling and the church was challenged for its life. Much of *Church Dogmatics* was written by Karl Barth in the midst and aftermath of Nazi persecution, genocide and aggression. Dietrich Bonhoeffer's theology and ethics rise out of his experience in a beleaguered underground seminary and latterly from a death cell.

It should occasion no wonder that churchmen are alive to questions about sexual behavior and family living in this era; for these are among the difficult and pressing issues of our day. The churches are relatively new at the job of addressing themselves to questions of sex, marriage and family life. You can search through the books on Christian ethics as late as the 1920's ("The Roaring Twenties," mind you) and find but scant reference to these ethical problems.

THEOLOGY AN AFTERTHOUGHT

Theology too often remains an afterthought to action. Revelation, coming as it does from relationships and the prayerful reading of history, seldom precedes the issues. For example, marriage must have been an organized and socially acceptable relationship for centuries before there were religious pronouncements about it. Any phenomenological examination of doctrine raises the assumption that the same condition must have also obtained for the family as an institution, for adultery as a transgression or divorce as an escape.

To admit that theology comes late into the investigations of issues is not to confess something disgraceful. We *need* time for reflection. The discovery of truth is almost always a slow process, painfully won. The disgraceful aspect, rather, is the avoidance of truth, and in this churchmen have often been guilty. Time and again we have turned our collective back on unsavory evidence of sexual behavior rather than face it. Thus when Alfred Kinsey and his research team published their finding that among the males studied 80 percent had experienced sexual intercourse before marriage, and that the average for all these males had been 330 experiences prior to marriage, churchmen denounced the researchers.

The study had included, among others, church-going men; and the data were unacceptable. Then when later the Kinsey team revealed their report on female behavior and its statistic that some 50 per cent of the women in their study had also experienced coitus before marriage, churchly anger was widespread. That the Masters and Johnson study, *Human Sexual Response*, raised less furor a decade later may owe more to the changing times than to maturing churchmen.

All truth is God's truth. Our need is less to fear truth than to pursue it. As the Calvinists staunchly maintain, truth is in order to goodness.

That puts a different light on our quest. It helps us to welcome contributions of the several disciplines to theology, which historically (and now perhaps ironically) is dubbed "the queen of sciences." More accurately put, theology is now a servant. Moreover, if truth itself, no matter how unpleasant it seems, is actually in order to goodness, then truth must have an influence on our ethical inquiry that naked fear cannot exert. Now that the fear approach to sexual morality no longer holds the power it once had (our population, for example, fears pregnancy and venereal infection less than formerly), we have been forced to turn to new and more theologically appropriate approaches in moral education. That, in part, is why churchmen appear confounded at this stage.

Our palpable frustration in relation to the truth about sex can be linked to the incompatibility of the findings of social science with our understanding of Christian tradition. However this is hardly the first time in history that churchmen have been stymied by inferences of the classical problem of reason and revelation. Nor does it promise to be the last. The church is gradually coming to a good conscience about accepting truth, i.e. God's truth, whether it shines through science or society or Holy Writ. We need to hear again that aphorism of Archbishop William Temple that God is at least as interested in the other areas of our life as he is in our religion.

Heavens! This could mean that God's disclosures might be expected to emanate from some extra-ecclesiastical events. The disclosures may not break forth from those improbable ivory-towered professional theologians at all, but from laymen. Laymen also happen to be theologians. It is impossible for the pewholders in any church to think about the meaning of sex, family or society without thinking (even unwittingly) theological thoughts.

JESUS CHRIST IS LORD

Even with theological uncertainty *vis-à-vis* our cultural crisis there are not a few doctrinal landmarks to which we can point. The foremost among these is that Jesus Christ is Lord of our life and of our times. His Lordship stands over our work and our decision making, over our sexuality, our getting and spending. We recall all too seldom that his Lordship reaches into all of our living, yes into our sexual concerns as well as into our prayer life.

Jesus as Lord offers us a norm of interpretation for life and conduct, with teachings about the Creator whose service is perfect freedom, and teachings about a Divine Word to know. If we cannot look to the teachings of Jesus for specific words about our specific sexual difficulties, we can look to him for a principle about ordering our sexual and family life within the Kingdom of God. Under the demand of the Kingdom, he makes clear, our sexual choice, our marriage and family life are to be disciplined. (Matt. 12:45ff., 19:12.)

It is this Christological emphasis that prevents us from heresy of assuming that we are the center of our universe. It is in his obedience that we find guidance for our own discipline in a commitment that changing times do not alter. For in Christ is revealed what we are to become: the new being. In his love ethic we see again the rule of the reborn, what classical theology has known as *usus in renatis*. Our calling in sexuality, to be a man or to be a woman, our calling in marital status to be a spouse or to be unwedded, our acceptance of ourselves as forgiven yet fallible creatures: all these are possible because of the Incarnation. As one church father phrased it, he became like us that we might become like him.

THE TRADITION

Christians have some of their worst moments when they cry like orphans of the storm that they have no tradition to guide them, no historic remembrance remaining. When they regard ethical problems as if they are altogether new, or as if these must be settled only in relation to the situation from which they arise, they ignore a priceless heritage. The church has been around for a long time and has gathered an impressive stock of wisdom along with her errors. Christianity did not begin with us and will not end with our end.

One way of being faithful to our Christian tradition may mean *not* repeating the past in detail. In point of fact, the reinterpretation of theology in new light is a solid portion of our tradition. The listening to prophetic innovation that inveighs against cultic orthodoxy is a time-honored exercise in Judaeo-Christian history. It teaches that we must also seek new light for our era.

Our tradition aids us in finding clues from the past, in avoiding the otherwise foredoomed practice of repeating historical mistakes, and in preventing us from weeping that we stand alone in time and space with our singular problems. We are moving in a great procession and with all its problems it offers a community of faith.

That tradition, in fact, aids us in realizing that the issue between the law and the Gospel is hardly new. External legal regulations are widely challenged in our day. But the church is not synonymous with prohibition. Although it is popularly tarred as the institution whose job it is to shout "Don't do that," the church actually affirms the nature and destiny of everyman, and his freedom too.

In its Victorian era, the church laid down the law quite punitively evidently on the assumption that to do otherwise was to encourage sin. Our era has worked hard to correct the excesses of Victorianism and has suffered some disappointment in the result. As Richard Unsworth observes, what has emerged from the cocoon of Victorianism is no butterfly but just a grubby moth. The way to throw off the bondage of the law is hardly to take on a new bondage of compulsive lawlessness. Between these two, as the Epistle to The Romans indicates, there is possible a responsible freedom. Sexual sins, be they fornication, adultery, or homosexuality are not considered either to be the worst nor the unforgivable in the catalogue of sins. There are, as Dorothy Sayers once reminded, six other deadly sins.

The law, regarded so warily by the new morality enthusiasts, does have its reasons for being. The law of love in particular has functions to educate, accuse and correct, to aid us in ordering our social responsibility, and to aid the faithful in their commitment. But the law does not usually succeed in reconciling persons. It does not always differentiate among people and their peculiar needs. It can be loveless if it is not touched by *agape* love. But with such love, it can redeem, it can guide, and can inform our institutions to bring aid to sinful and unreliable human weakness.

Any new formulation of sexual ethic is going to have to face up to the need for law, not a legalism which is dehumanizing and excessively scrupulous, but as a support and in sympathy for persons.

OUR VOCATION

The *Imago Dei* doctrine reminds us that we are all, male and female, created in the image of God. Our understanding of our own sexuality is hidden in God in whom we live and move and have our being.

It is our sexuality that aids us in being genuinely human, that forms the most profound aspect of our personality. But the genuine human experience does not depend upon performing the coital act. This truth can be affirmed for the unmarried, yes, for Jesus himself. Everyone is a psychosexual person. In biblical thought you *are* your body.

But it may be a fallacy to assume that sexuality is understood only through complete candor, the open, frank talk and revelation that characterizes much of our modern conversation, literature, and entertainment. There is also a mystery about the sexual which is essential to its understanding.

When we lose our way a large part of our trouble stems from forgetting our theological directional signals. We sometimes struggle to work out our salvation as if everything depends on us. It is then that once again we must recollect that we did not choose but were chosen. We are not wholly responsible for locating meaning in life. God has sent meaning into our midst, ordering both our creation and our redemption. He has spoken to us through his Son in the Incarnation.

We have a destination whose maker and builder is God. And, as the Apostle Paul writes, we are predestined. But predestination does not mean, as many argue, that we are somehow predetermined by our past. Instead it means that we are directed toward the future. That is we can be justified by faith (the future) rather than by works (the past). This is our teleological (that is, goal-directed) orientation because God has given our lives a purpose. Moreover it is eschatological, i.e. it has an unfolding solution at the end where God is in charge.

Our times are in his hands. Surely our sex-saturated culture, surely our rapid social change, surely our moral challenge have not defeated almighty God. We live *sub specie eternitatis*, under the aspect of eternity. In these events of our muddled current history we may discern God's will for our times, find his often unwelcome truth for our day and grope our way to new obedience.

2

Sexuality and Responsibility: A New Phase

•

HARVEY GALLAGHER COX, JR.

Ever provocative in his writing, Harvey G. Cox here lampoons (among other excesses) the sexual technicians, marriage manuals and counselors whose appearance testifies to society's preoccupation with sex. The professor of divinity at Harvard Divinity School is author of *Festivity and Fantasy, The Secular City, On Not Leaving It To The Snake, God's Revolution and Man's Responsibility* and editor of two other books, *The Church Amid Revolution* and *The Situation Ethics Debate.*

●

THERE IS INCREASING EVIDENCE from every side that churches and Christian groups all over the world are engaging in a searching and thorough re-examination of their understanding of sexuality. From England there came the thoughtful paper *Towards a Quaker View of Sex* composed by members of the Society of Friends in an effort to answer questions posed them by sincere young members of their community. This paper opens a whole new way of thinking and talking about sexuality and is a refreshing change from most of the literature we have seen in the field. From a group of concerned Christians in State College, Pennsylvania, comes a book entitled *Honest Sex* and sub-titled *A Study by and for Adult Christians* but nicknamed "The Sycamore Report" after the name of the group which had prepared it. From the Vatican there comes repeated word of serious reconsideration by Roman Catholic theologians of their church's prohibition of so-called artificial methods of contraception. From The Group for the Advancement of Psychiatry there comes a book on *Sex and the College Student* which reflects deep theological insight into the relationship between maturation and freedom to choose responsibly one's own way in sexual behavior. In short the door has now been opened for a broader, deeper and more candid conversation among Christians about sexuality than had seemed possible just a few years previously.

We should be grateful for the openness and candor with which this discussion is going on. Certainly the matter of sexuality is a deeply important one and one about which the church should never remain eternally and uncritically fixed in a particular stance. However we should also notice that the focus of the secular discussion about sexuality is shifting so rapidly that it is difficult for the church and for Christian thinkers to remain in touch with it. There is frequently a tendency for the discussion in the church to reflect a previous stage of the discussion outside the church and therefore to have only marginal reference to the frontier points of the secular discussion.

In this paper I wish to deal with four points of discussion in our contemporary North American society on the matter of sexuality. There are four areas which I believe reflect the next stage of the discussion and for which there is at the moment relatively little consideration within the churches themselves. I do believe however that the Christian gospel and the biblical tradition underlying it have much that is extraordinarily valuable to contribute to these questions. There remains only the task of understanding the dynamics lying behind these questions, both the psychological, sociological and theological ingredients of the questions, and the appropriate ways of dealing with them from a biblical perspective.

I shall group these questions under four headings entitled:

1. The question of *competence.*
2. The problems arising from a view of sexuality as *compensation.*
3. The crisis posed for *communication* by certain contemporary practices in sexuality.
4. The new *compulsions* in the field of sexual behavior.

COMPETENCE

Under *competence* I refer to the massive new knowledge of sexual techniques and physiology made available to us by modern science and mass media. Certainly there was an important need to acquire competence in our knowledge of sexuality and this need remains a very important one. We should not for a moment call for a return to the superstition, ignorance and obscurantism which frequently characterized our attitudes toward sexuality in the past. However, to recognize the advantages of competence and knowledge does not in any way diminish the problems which this increased competence brings with it. Psychologists and psychiatrists especially on college campuses now frequently report that student and faculty clients come to them with a very different complaint than those brought fifteen years ago. The psychiatrists say that

these people today frequently complain that sex experience has
little or no meaning for them, that what they had expected to be
an intensely pleasurable and psychologically fulfilling activity turns
out to be "a letdown" or "there's just nothing to it." Many times
clients talk about the fact that their sexual partners do not seem
to be enjoying the activity and therefore they do not enjoy it themselves. Sometimes they suggest that the other person doesn't "seem
to be there"—"is not present."

This series of complaints is a very different one than the problems brought just a few years ago by students whose main difficulties in the area of sexuality were how to deal with the restraints
and inhibitions inherited from their parental training.

It is difficult to say precisely how much of the "new neurosis"
can be attributed to the increase in competence. Some observers,
however, have contended that where competence reaches such a
high level, any kind of apprehensiveness or wonder disappears.
The activity is itself shorn of some of its essential features. This
theme is one which is now beginning to occupy the attention
of some of our most sensitive artists. Several years ago a young
Polish film maker produced a film entitled *The Innocent Magi-
cians*. It told the story of a young doctor who was also a jazz musi-
cian in his spare time living in a bachelor's apartment in modern
Warsaw. He was portrayed as the typical competent, confident
and even cocksure contemporary urban man for whom sexuality
held absolutely no terrors. One evening he picked up an attractive
girl at a night club and they returned to his apartment. At that
point it became clear that the girl herself also has the same personality characteristics of the doctor. She surprises him by suggesting that if they were now to proceed with the standard seduction
scene they really ought to do it according to the rules. She then
puts a large paper chart on the wall and each of them begins to
make contributions to the scenario that they will follow. They
write the various steps that will ensue: for example (1) pour a
drink (2) soft music on the record player (3) remove shoes (4)
second drink (5) a kiss, etc. They then begin to act out the scenario they have contrived, judging each other on their respective

performances. The film is a hilarious and tragic commentary on the ultra self-consciousness of these two young people in the field of sexuality. Eventually in this film the self-consciousness breaks down and an element of human spontaneity intrudes. However, the warning of the film seems clear. The value of candor and competence being undeniable, nevertheless they carry with them their own dangers in the lack of immediacy and spontaneity.

This issue of the relationship between feeling and competence applies not only to sexuality but to a large number of different issues in the world influenced by technology. In a way it is the same issue faced by theological students who must learn how to analyze the phenomenon of prayer and still be able to pray, engage in historical and literary criticism of the Bible and yet somehow find the Bible able to speak to them. There aren't many people who believe that these two activities are mutually contradictory and competence and feeling cannot go together. I do not personally hold this opinion but I believe that increased competence and consciousness do provide problems in the achievement of sexual fulfillment in human beings which must be dealt with. It also seems to me that a biblical view of the nature of man, and of his communities and of his relationships to his fellow creatures should be able to make a contribution to this characteristically contemporary problem in human sexuality. Unfortunately not very much has been done to respond to this issue. Most of the writing about sexuality from Christians either merely encourages further candor and further self-consciousness on the one hand, or condemns this kind of development of competence on the other without recognizing that both competence and companionship are essential ingredients in sexuality and that these are not necessarily mutually exclusive.

COMPENSATION

Another serious issue in human sexuality is that many people now turn to sexuality as a *compensation* for the increased difficulty of human participation in technological and political life. Sex becomes a vehicle for the expression of intimate and elemental emotion to the degree that the organization of society squeezes out intimacy and warmth through the process of rationalization. Also as politics become more distant and more specialized and as people feel increasingly alienated from their political communities they tend to turn to sexuality as a way of expressing personhood and a type of minuscule community as a substitute for political community. There is a real danger that this movement will both demand too much of human sexuality and also see it as less important than it really is in other ways.

No one can deny that the tendency of modern society is toward the rationalization of the organization of human work. Especially the impact of computers has among other things forced us to take a hard look at the random and singular aspects of the work relationship and to try to quantify elements which have up until now been incapable of quantification. One good example of how the rationalization of work removes certain human relationships with sexual overtones is the development of the "secretarial pool." Formerly the relationship between a man and his secretary although it could be difficult and tension-ridden at least had a certain continuing human quality. Efficiency and higher cost however require sharing of secretarial services and the pooling of skills such that the old-fashioned relationship between the executive and his secretary is now often diminished if not discarded. Examples could be multiplied of this type of dehumanization of the work relationship and it often leads to compensation in other areas. However this expectation of compensation in other areas frequently puts an undue strain on the sexuality there and causes difficulties.

In the area of political life the problem is an even more unsettling one. The failure of our society to provide adequate political mechanisms and instrumentalities for facilitating popular participation in a technological culture has produced an element of alienation from the political system and suspicion and distrust of its possibilities. The retreat from politics can often express itself in a compensating overemphasis on the private and intimate sphere. Once again this could have disastrous consequences both because of the overload of expectations placed on the private sphere and because it tends to exempt the political community from the essential criticism, interest and participation of those who flee to privatization.

The Christian understanding of man places him squarely in a community. It knows no doctrine of man which will allow for a simple retreat to private life, ignoring public communities and responsibilities. Its view of sexuality therefore cannot condone a compensatory understanding of sex that would allow for this kind of depoliticization of man's role in the world. Christians must raise serious questions about sex compensation. We do so not to denigrate sex but to guard the importance of political community. Unfortunately our criticism of this privatization of man may be misunderstood as a criticism of sexuality itself or of the freedom and openness of sexuality which is a positive characteristic of the modern world. We should try to avoid this but we should not allow the possibility of being misunderstood to deter us from raising serious questions about the misuse of sexuality as a way of retreating from and avoiding the difficulties of the larger political environment.

COMMUNICATION

Since sexuality is at least in part a style of *communication*, Christians have some concern about protecting this form of communication from forces which might tend to weaken or distort it. The issue of sexuality as communication has been raised very forcibly in the writings of George Steiner. In an article entitled "Night Words" (*Encounter*, October 1965) the distinguished writer and critic, Mr. Steiner, asks some pertinent questions about the liberal assumption, shared also by many modern Christians, that published clinical descriptions not only of sex but of sadism and perversion must be defended and upheld in the name of freedom. He suggests that the torrent of pornography has now reached a point where we must ask whether it is really worth defending any more. He asks the question not because he is intent on upholding some moral law but because he wants to protect the privacy of the words human beings use in their most intimate moments, the "night words." Steiner therefore questions the idea of "total statement" both from the literary and the human perspective, and suggests that we have lived through too much actual sadism in our century to waste much energy defending and encouraging its literary description. He feels that the contemporary obsession with detailed clinical descriptions of sex (in contrast to the thrilling and engaging but skillful and indirect way it was dealt with by, say Tolstoy or Eliot) may signify a "massive onslaught on human privacy," a real and present endangering of "the delicate processes by which we seek to become our singular selves, to hear the echo of our specific being." He argues that sexual relations, especially in an era of massive and pervasive *publicity*, should be a citadel of privacy. Sexuality should be guarded as "the nightplace where we must be allowed to gather the splintered and harried elements of our consciousness to some kind of inviolate order and repose."

How is that last sanctuary of privacy faring against the onslaught of those who would make it public? A writer in *Esquire* comments on this question in a recent issue devoted in part to a discussion of sex. He claims that the sex technologists, manual writers and performance measurers have overpopulated our bedrooms, that the supremely private act is being ruined by too much analysis and description.

Steiner is afraid that this exposure of sexuality to "publicification" contributes to the withering of our capacity to feel and to experience. He says a totalitarian society, whether its standards are imposed by a Gestapo or by mass media, can afford to allow no areas of life to escape from its standardization and control. He concludes that the worst present danger to our inward freedom is not either external censorship or verbal reticence. It lies rather in the facile contempt which the erotic novelist exhibits for his readers, for his personages, and for the language. Our dreams are marketed wholesale.

George Steiner's discussion creates a particularly tricky problem for Christian ethics. For so long Christian moralists have opposed the freedom of writers to describe the sexual life that it would seem ill advised for us to begin to use the same arguments and rhetoric again. However, our recent uncritical endorsement and even celebration of the so-called new freedom of the writer is also something that needs serious questioning. If it is true, as Steiner claims, that a misuse of the language of intimacy can result in the endangering of intimacy itself then we should deplore the way in which the most intimate phases of human life are subjected to over-publicity. The question however, now becomes one of taste and discrimination rather than a question of censorship and prohibition. It is a question of how the important and interesting dimension of man's life which we call the sexual can be depicted and eluded in writing, such that our minds and spirits are stretched and our imagination stimulated, without contributing to the destruction of that inner citadel of freedom which is so important especially in an era in which so much of our lives have no real privacy. Christian moralists should walk with a special wariness on this subject recognizing how badly we have often performed in the past, by insisting that such masterpieces of literature as *Ulysses* by James Joyce and *Madame Bovary* by Gustave Flaubert were unworthy pieces of literature. I do not believe that Christians should advocate precensorship or the prohibition of any work of art, short story, picture or novel however questionable it may seem to us. We have erred too frequently in the past to allow ourselves to be the judges of another man's conscience. This is why I recently contributed to an advertisement protesting the cruel five-year imprisonment of Mr. Ralph Ginsburg, the Editor of *Eros* magazine.

I do not believe however that our commitment to the freedom of publication necessarily means that we must find value or celebrate the merits of the material whose publication we have defended. I believe that Christians should be just as vigorous in criticizing the deplorable taste, bad writing, and dehumanizing effects of much of the contemporary flood of pornographic literature as anyone else. We do this however by pointing out its weaknesses and by encouraging the production of better and more adequate depictions of human life, not by preventing its publica-

tion. Also we object to it not because of some shrinking violet attitude about what should or should not be published but because
we have an unswerving commitment to the protection of intimacy
and privacy in human life.

COMPULSION

Despite the reports to the contrary there are still large elements
of *compulsion* in the sexual life of modern human beings which
militate against maturity, freedom and fulfillment in community.
There are many mistaken observers who wrongly feel that since
churchly prohibition and theological rulings now exert less influence, people are therefore freer in their sexual lives. Margaret
Mead in an address at Radcliffe College pointed out that there are
still compulsive pressures in the culture forcing people to make
decisions about sexuality which are not according to their own free
choice. It is certainly true that in many colleges the girl who remains a virgin is the one who must defend her choice against the
criticisms and pressures of her friends rather than vice versa. As
one writer recently expressed it, "the old commandment Thou
Shalt Not has now been replaced by an equally strident Thou
Shalt!"

Clearly the Christian gospel calls men into freedom and away
from the bondage of any kind of depersonalizing legalism. It op-
poses both the unqualified Thou Shalt Not and the equally unqualified Thou Shalt. It insists that human beings in order to be
full human beings in the sight of God must themselves choose
their own modes of sexual expression and participation. They do
this of course in responsibility to their fellow human beings and
within a culture which spells out the images, metaphors and values
by which sexuality is understood. However, in the final analysis
man not only believes and dies for himself, as Luther says; man
also develops his characteristic style of sexuality on his own.

It is particularly unfortunate that as the new legalism of the
Thou Shalt begins to make such an impact on our younger generation that certain of the mass media organs still believe that the

major pressure operative in our sexual lives are the old prohibitions, the Thou Shalt Not. *Playboy* magazine is a very good example of the fascination of a particular generation of young Americans with a set of prohibitions which are now virtually inoperative in our culture; at the same time these young people harp constantly on the superannuated prohibitions while in effect acting as the spokesmen for the new legalism of conformity.

The danger that the church faces here however, is that it will be tempted to respond to the new legalism of Thou Shalt in a negative rather than in a positive way. It will be tempted to recur to the old legalism of the Thou Shalt Not rather than countering the new legalism with the gospel which transcends both the Thou Shalt and the Thou Shalt Not with the call to freedom and responsibility in community. Again in this regard it is particularly difficult for the church to be a part of the discussion since its voice has so often been raised in the name of ancient legalisms that when it criticizes contemporary legalisms it will almost certainly be misunderstood to be advocating the return to the old ones.

There is also a serious question about whether it is even possible to talk about sexuality in freedom and responsibility without an element of coercion and compulsion. There are important thinkers including Sigmund Freud who believe that civilization itself depends on the repression and sublimation of sexual tendencies and without a structure of sublimation civilization would not be possible. Some of Freud's successors believe that this type of coercive and repressive culture is not essential but that we can develop modes of self-expression which preserve the integrity of the self but do not destroy the culture system which is also essential to human life.

The theological question involved here is whether it is that of maturity. To what extent should the Christian gospel function as one of the symbolic modes of repression and sublimation in our society and to what extent should it assume that other modalities of repression will continue to function even though it no longer plays that particular cultural role. This question is closely related to the whole complex discussion about the end of the age of Constantine and the liberation of the church from its need to function as the sacral legitimator of Western Christian culture. It may be that the Christian gospel is now entering a period in which its focus will be on human community and fulfillment of the self within human community with less emphasis on the cementing and sacrilizing of whole civilization and cultural systems. In part this question also raises the issue of eschatology that is, whether we experience in this life and on this earth some of the promise of the gospel that he who is freed from the bondage of the law can live according to the spirit. There are schools of theology especially those arising from the Protestant Reformation which severely criticize any suggestion that this eschatological promise is anything but futuristic. There are other traditions represented by the sectarian history of Christianity which suggest that there are at least elements of eschatological fulfillment and therefore freedom from external compulsion within history itself.

CONCLUSION

These four issues, competence, compensation, communication and compulsion signify the agenda of Christian theological concern about human sexuality and family life in our time. It is true that most of our discussion in the church has not focused on any one of these issues with much regularity or depth. It is also true that by focusing on them we may often appear to be taking a step back from the atmosphere of openness and sexual freedom which characterizes our time and which many churchmen rightly feel they should support against the repressions of the past. However, the courage to deal with contemporary issues honestly and forthrightly regardless of the danger of being misunderstood either from the right or from the left should be our main inspiration and should deliver us from the fear of being wrongly categorized by those with other axes to grind, so that we can discuss with candor and reverence that element of human life which shines our personhood at its very center.

3

The Outlook for an Adequate Ethic

•

GIBSON WINTER

The crisis in sexual relationships is rooted in a struggle for personal integrity within a technological society: this is one hypothesis of Gibson Winter in the pages that follow. Dr. Winter is professor of ethics and society at The Divinity School, The University of Chicago. He has written *Love and Conflict, The Suburban Captivity Of The Churches, The New Creation As Metropolis,* and *Elements For A Social Ethic.* He edited the collection *Social Ethics: Issues In Ethics And Society.*

•

PERHAPS OUR MOST SERIOUS current problem is to assess the seriousness of the crisis in sexual relationships on our continent. How radical is the change in these relationships? How pressing are the uncertainties with which young people, married couples and parents are struggling? Is this largely a crisis created by the mass media which now create markets and publics by disposing of God in one series and creating a panic over LSD in the next? My own conviction is that beneath the publicists' crisis there are serious issues, however badly defined by the media; our task is to clarify and identify these issues in a responsible way.

THE PERSONAL AGE IN SEXUALITY

When we consider the changes which we are experiencing, the most obvious fact is the transformation of the sexual sphere into a more private concern. The culture of sexuality is changing, particularly for the younger generation. We all know that the selection of marital partners, the maintenance of marital relationships and the role of the family in the society have gradually been transformed from public to somewhat more private questions in the last century. Dietrich Von Oppen titled his book, *The Personal Age*. That phrase applies even more to the sphere with which we are concerned; we live now in The Personal Age in Sexuality. This may seem paradoxical since advertising and ventures such as *Playboy* seem to be making sexuality an even more objective, commercial, marketable object. Despite these hangovers from the rapidly disappearing culture of a productive age, the struggle of the youth culture is to make sexually qualified relationships authentically personal. Whatever the aberrations of the younger group in this field, they are seeking to wrest sexuality from the grip of outmoded authorities and the exploitation of a commercial age. The

38

shift of the sexual province of meaning to the personal and private sphere means that traditional law and external sanctions have an entirely different function; inherited notions of chastity and threats of disease, pregnancy or censure no longer suffice to establish a morality of sexual relationships. Personal responsibility is going to be the essence of any morality of sex in our time, which means that personal integrity and mutual fulfillment through the continuity of relationships will have to determine appropriate rules and relevant sanctions. We may spend a lot of time in our deliberations talking laws, sanctions and obligations to external authorities—human or divine—but this will be rhetoric largely for our own gratification and quite irrelevant to the issues at hand. Rules of the game are needed, but we shall have to seek them as guides and supports for personal responsibility. Hence, our basic task is to grasp the criteria of personal responsibility in this sphere.

The Personal Age in Sexuality confronts us with the deeper question of what stake we have in the traditional middle-class ethic of sexuality? In what sense is this ethic intrinsic to our religio-ethical tradition? Put another way, does the new sexual culture disclose more substantive personal and social values in our religious tradition which were obscured by the age of production and its middle-class ethic?

The shift to the Personal Age in Sexuality clearly confronts us with basic questions about the nature and continuity of marital relationships. A complex society creates many problems for the personal and communal sphere of activities, but it also brings this sphere to light and frees it for authentic development. It is time we rethought the nature of marital relationships and found some guide lines for this struggle to reform our divorce laws. Marriage obviously impinges upon the public sphere; legal accountability has to be maintained on appropriate levels; however, the essence of marriage is the quality of the relationship between the persons, and this falls within the private sphere of moral obligation. We need to explore the constitution of a marriage, the sources of its continuity and power, and come to some understanding of the stake which our religio-ethical tradition has in continuity for its own sake. Here more than anywhere else our pastors and residential congregations need some clearer vision of the ministry of the churches to marital and parental relationships.

The emergence of the Personal Age in Sexuality also means that the family bears an increasing burden for the society in cultivating personal integrity, social flexibility and cultural aptitude in the citizens. Our struggle with education makes it increasingly evident that personal and cultural background in the family is essential to participation in a complex, high technology society. It is also becoming evident that a family which is dominated by career and consumer values, the reflex of a commercial, productive age, constitutes an inadequate community for such a difficult task. Here the younger generation point us toward the public corollary to the Personal Age, an increasing emphasis on participation and public service. A Personal Age in Sexuality can only emerge with increasing concern for participation in the public sphere; otherwise, the personal sphere degenerates into privatized preoccupation with emotional experiences. It becomes an autistic age. Moreover, the family can only carry this burden for the society in a technological era as it is sustained and supported by economic security and support. The discussion of Guaranteed Income is pointing in this direction. We need to become clear on the prerequisites in economic security with which every member of a complex society has to be endowed in order to exercise initiative and personal freedom. Our productive age assumed that individuals and families could earn membership in the society through the exercise of freedom. In a technological age, membership cannot be earned, because those who are excluded from its prerequisites at birth can never make up the gap in technological and cultural participation. Personal freedom in the new age requires a prior sharing in the economic, social and cultural facilities with which the society is endowed. In this sense, the Personal Age in Sexuality has its counterpart in the Emergence of the Social Man. The family as community of the private sphere is, thus, dependent first upon the facilities which the society owes it in order that the society may continue to develop in the direction of cultural enrichment and public responsibility. We speak here of *rights to participation in the society*, but our social ethic is sadly deficient in even reflecting on this problem. If we are concerned about the family, this is part of our task.

These problems are immense and far-ranging. They bring the whole force of an organizational society to the bar of judgment. We can be sure, by the interrelated nature of our world, that a crisis in the sexual sphere betokens a fundamental crisis in our culture. We shall have to come to terms with that cultural crisis and engage in a theological critique of our culture. Sexuality is the substratum of the social process, because it reflects our dependence upon one another, the anxiety of our distance from one another and the unifying power of love in opening communication, generating community and evoking the commitments through which societal fulfillment finds embodiment in history. Hence, the preoccupations which trouble us—our desperate entrapment in Vietnam, the inequity of our Selective Service structure, the ghettos which manifest the brutality of a productive society and its disregard for the person, our internal bleeding over racial inequities that go back over centuries, the imbalance of power between Canada and the United States, and the lack of clear lines for a dialogue with Latin America—all of these concerns are refracted in their own way through the issues that arise in the sexual sphere. Our limited task is to see these problems through the prism of the sexually qualified relationships—to discern our interdependence in life and to fashion a clearer vision of our commitments.

RECOGNIZING A REVOLUTION

The notion that we are in the midst of a sexual revolution is a hypothesis. If the hypothesis is sound, a revolution in sexual morality has been in the making for many years and is only now becoming evident. Furthermore, if such a revolution is under way, a major aspect of our task is to identify and understand this revolutionary process.

There are various ways in which we can recognize a revolution. We sense revolutionary upheavals through certain kinds of change, through strains to which people are subjected, through awareness of ferment and through a sense of normlessness. I have suggested that we are moving into a Personal Age in the sphere of sexuality, by which I meant that sexuality was being unraveled from our public, institutional life and becoming an area of personal or private activity; it is also a vehicle for a humanistic revolt against an organizational society. The sexual sphere has become a major locus of the search for human values in our complex, high technology society.

Why should the sexual sphere become a vehicle for a search for human values? Many people feel that sexuality has become a commercial instrument or merely a sign of the corruption of our society. How could this sphere of activity assume such central significance in our cultural development?

The search for human values has been pressed with increasing urgency in Western culture during these centuries of technological development. In Europe, this search found radical expression in the existentialist movement. One focus of the search in the United States has been the human rights movement; indeed, the rights movement can best be understood as a struggle for a participatory democracy in which the human values of freedom and consent gain full play. In the ghetto, for example, a struggle is under way against domination by welfare bureaucracies. This is an assertion of personal rights and dignity. The Students for a Democratic Society have spearheaded this thrust toward participation and consent. In each of these movements, there is a struggle for authentic personhood against the claims of massive organizations. My hypothesis about the sexual revolution, therefore, is that sexuality is a major locus of the struggle for personal values against organizational control in our society. This coincidence of the personal age in sexuality and the broad search for human values in the society is generating a sexual revolution which is both threatening and promising for our moral and cultural development.

We live in a society of massive organizational structures. This is a bureaucratic society. In acknowledging this, we can appreciate the depth of the struggle for human values in the society without falling into the error of imagining that such organizations can simply be wished away. One cannot organize a complex, highly interdependent society without rational structures. This is what we really mean by bureaucracy—the rationalization of organization. It is a structure which increases predictability and control. In order to gain this kind of predictability, activities have to be schematized. However, in a bureaucratic society people feel that they are objects which are manipulated by impersonal organizations. They feel a loss of integrity.

Some of our industrial leaders are aware of this depersonalizing force of massive organization; they are working to broaden levels of personal responsibility and enhance a sense of participation. Rapid improvement in our technology of communication may make it possible to increase the scope of responsibility on various levels of organization, although the initial tendency has been to increase centralization of control. Whatever the direction of this process in coming decades, and it is one of our most critical problems, large segments of our society *feel* that they are objects of welfare bureaucracies or educational machines. This is especially true of the powerless in the ghettos and the youth who are being prepared to participate in the organizational society. These are two major elements of the powerless mass in a technological society.

The waves of protest in recent decades, both among students and in the ghettos, reflect a struggle against powerlessness; these protests also disclose the profound human struggle for dignity and participation which characterizes our era.

The sexual sphere has become a locus for exploration of personal values in this organizational society because sexuality is a sphere in which the powerless still have some voice. Sexuality often becomes a way of compensating for personal impoverishment; and compensatory sexuality can endanger the sexual maturity of many adults. However, I am also suggesting that sexuality is an alternative way of working at authentic human values in the society—the achievement of consent, freedom and participation.

I would draw here an analogy to the role of poetic activity in the Soviet culture. In the Soviet culture there is a struggle going on for liberty, but the political structure is so rigidly bureaucratized that it offers a poor vehicle in the struggle for human liberty. We look too simply at other cultures from our American experience with its own particular environment and historical destiny. We expect the struggle for freedom to be political and economic. In the Soviet Union, if I read this right, the poetic, humanistic sphere is the field in which the struggle for human liberty is being worked out. This is an alternative path to the political, but a valid path.

Both sexuality and poetic are dangerous to a society. These are powerful expressions of human creativity. Plato was sensitive to the threat of the poets to social stability. They create trouble, they change the language, they create new symbols. This is also happening in the transformation of the culture of sexuality. A new style of human authenticity is being sought in the sexual sphere of our experience. The poetic in the Soviet experience and the sexual in our own experience are beachheads for social and cultural revolution.

In that context, we should recognize the ambiguity of revolutions of this kind. Plato was not entirely wrong about the poets. These things are dangerous to public order; he was, perhaps, too preoccupied with order, because he believed that he had a vision of the true order and Athenian society needed stability. We also cherish stability, and this marks the danger of the sexual revolution.

There is a search for personal values in the sexual sphere. I call this the emerging Personal Age in Sexuality. There is an attempt to regain that which is alienated. Under the disciplines of the Protestant ethic, our bodies were alienated from us. The sexual revolution seeks the recovery of embodied life. The body is not the enemy; it is not to be kept in a dark corner. This leads us back to Freud. We see Freud as a prophetic voice, because Freud's real concern was to unify man's rationality and his body, to overcome the disjunction of the body and mind or body and spirit.

However, the sexual revolution is also aggression against the society. It is a way for the young people to get even with us, if you want to put it in terms of the young; it is also the way a husband gets even with his wife, or a wife gets even with her husband. With these deep, vital forces, the search for reunion may also be alienating and antagonistic, because this kind of love and conflict is built into the fabric of our existence.

Hence, the revolt of the powerless, and we are all powerless in a society of this scope and magnitude, becomes an act of aggression as well as search. The mimeographed poem circulating from dacha to dacha around Moscow is an act of aggression as well as search for authentic values. This is like a bomb plot; it destroys the order which is imposed and opens up the possibility of a new order. We need to be sensitive to the depths, the ambiguity of this kind of revolution. In one sense, one could say that the sexual sphere is the vehicle of revolt for the bureaucratic proletariat; these are the powerless in a high technology society. This is the ambiguity of the revolution.

I want to stress the creative aspect of this revolution. I also want to keep its socially destructive dimensions as a backdrop. The same holds for the rights movement. The rights movement has within it this same ambiguity: to lie down in front of a bus is to demonstrate (I say this now as a demonstrator) one's convictions, to affirm that one participates in this society and in its struggle for rights; it is also a way of getting even with the establishment. I want to talk on the positive side of this revolt. We are committed to the Civil Rights revolution in the public sphere and to the sexual revolution in the private sphere as vehicles of search for a more human and a more adequate society. These are broadly parallel commitments. They are dangerous commitments. They are commitments to the transformation of a society which is in danger of becoming a bureaucratic nightmare of increasing uniformity.

THE RECOVERY OF SEXUALITY'S MEANING

The recovery of sexuality is part of our salvation—an aspect of wholeness. It is a promise now of wholeness that has before us the promise of fulfillment and meaning. The work of liberation has to come first. The search for an ethic, a style, a code, if you will, has to come in the process. This is a serious and difficult business.

We do not choose our destinies. We do not choose the time in which we live. We do not choose the form in which the struggle for freedom, equality, consent and brotherhood is to be waged. Ours is a period in which this struggle will take place politically in the field of rights and personally in the field of sexual wholeness. Our destiny is to struggle for the meaning of our faith and the meaning of our freedom within these two revolutions. These are not new revolutions. They have been centuries in the making. We certainly have come to a pivotal point, to a *kairos* in our own time. We may not see resolutions of these struggles. Our obedience is given in these spheres; the search for humanness in our society will occur in these spheres.

We are moving out of an achievement culture. The middle-class style is important for this kind of culture, but we are moving out of it. We are moving toward a different kind of family. The Students for a Democratic Society, by and large, are youngsters from middle-class families who have been brought up in a much more democratic home than most of their forebears dreamed of. These youngsters have tasted democracy at home; they will not tolerate a society in which so many are excluded from democracy. Those S.D.S. kids in the dirty clothes, sneakers and beards are our children; they have experienced democracy and they want society to experience it. They are not going to give up until society does experience it.

There is a fabric to the middle-class ethic. We are not throwing this out; we are humanizing it, democratizing it, enriching it. Our culture needs to be enriched. But how is it being enriched by the recovery of the sexual sphere? It is being enriched by acknowledging man's embodiment. To say that man is an embodied being is to claim that he has finite freedom, contingent being-in-the-world, that he belongs to nature, the universe, the creation. To say that you belong to nature means that nature is built into you, that it is reflected in you, that your body is your openness on the universe and the world, and that this is the world to which you belong.

This, as I read him, is what Paul Tillich was saying to our world. Being, life, nature, vitality is the creation of cultural, social, and natural universes, taking them into the realm of spirit. Essentially, this power is love, the freeing and unifying power of our being. Sexuality is the somatic expression of our belonging to the universe, of our belonging to one another; a power which prevents us from living in isolation, which reflects itself in our dependence on one another. At the same time, this power places us against one another, separates us from one another in the particularity of our own bodily experience. In this new anthropology (and I think we are moving toward a new Christian anthropolgy in our time) we are going to be a lot more optimistic, especially about the creative and reconciling power of our embodiment. Sin will still be reckoned with in this anthropology. But sin will be seen in the unity of the person. Sin is not a matter of physical passions. Sin is the total person over against his total world, and redemption is the fulfillment of the whole, embodied personality. We can only affirm the disclosure of sexuality because it belongs to our fulfillment. The renewal of the bodily, the struggle for the renewal of our whole being, becomes a crucial area in which we will work and struggle. This is not the time for premature prescriptive statements, even though the churches and the society expect guide lines. This is the time to enlarge the breadth of this experience, the cultural and symbolic, as well as the physical, levels of sexuality. This is the time for *inquiry*. This is the time for *research*, for openness, for humility. This is the time to identify our experiences. As Roy Fairchild has said, "We do not even have the words to identify many of the things which we have experienced." We have so suppressed the sexual sphere that we lack words with which to express the sexual qualification of our lives. The things that are important to a society have a rich vocabulary, whether camels in the Middle East or corn in the Indian societies. Where a society has a rich experience, it elaborates its vocabulary, because we can have experiences through symbols. Ours is the time for search, description, formulation, identification in human relationships.

WORSHIP AND MINISTRY

This touches the problem of worship in the contemporary world. It is almost impossible, in my opinion, for contemporary man to worship. He is struggling with the meaning of symbol and ritual, because his preoccupation with technology has flattened his world and emptied it of mystery. Our concern with sexuality extends to the whole of man's being. We have pushed the religious out, because we have suppressed the personal. It is not God who is dead but man who is dying. It is even debatable whether one can have a religious experience in our time. When we talk about the recovery of feelings, of embodiment, of the expressive reality of existence, we are talking about the possibility of being religious in an authentic sense. The religiousness which we have is alien to our search for the fully human. Body and spirit belong together. What God has joined together, let no man put asunder. So far as the sexual revolution is an authentic search for the wholeness of man and his personal community, it is a genuine expression of our Jewish and Christian heritage. With all its dangers, this revolution has a rightful claim on our ministries and service.

A true ethic is a style that maintains the expression of love. Our creative forces are chaotic. These forces are dangerous. They need channels to order them and to sustain their creative possibilities. But an ethic has to grow out of life; it has to be a style appropriate to our own experience. My argument is that the church has always known that an ethic is shaped by the experiences and actions of people. This is what the confessional is about, a place to consider and shape our experience. The church's pastoral ministry is where its ethic is to be fashioned. The lived experience of relationships furnishes the materials of ethical evaluation, but the ethical style has to be adequate to the experience. Our tradition has to be reshaped in the light of experience. Our tradition judges this experience, but we transform the tradition by the claims of experience. This is the dialectic of man's historical being and his ethic. Man never has an order which is suitable to that moment which he is constituting. In this sense, the Gospel always liberates us from the past for the present. We are always constituting and reconstituting our ethic. The theologians and ethicists can be useful as participants in this process. They can help to clarify our experience from the tradition, to evaluate, to shape and to point toward that which we are living with and that which we are experiencing.

In a period of rapid social change such as this, ethical patterns also change. We think they are changing rapidly. Even if a pattern changes the slightest bit, we feel as if everything is up for grabs. In this kind of period, if we are going to work at the problem of an ethic, we first have to participate in these changing cultures. We have to participate in the youth culture, in the personal sphere of family problems. We have to listen, we have to be part of this culture. If we are going to work at ethics, we are going to work at what it means to live as a human being with a human style of life in a technological society. This is the church's task.

Some conservatives are troubled by those of us who criticize the churches. They say that we "climinate" the congregation. That is not what we are saying at all. We are saying, get with the action! If a church structure is no good, forget it! Make a new structure that enables you to participate in the society. Congregations are suitable structures to deal with this personal sphere of exploration of human values. Let's use them for this task.

In a complex society, we need scientific research as well as pastoral ministry. In the complex period, we need the sciences to accumulate more data and to generalize our experience. We always take our own experience as general and say this is what is happening. That may be true. It may not!

To evaluate both our experience and our tradition means that we bring in the evaluative and the normative, not as alien structures that we want to impose but as integral to this process of discovery.

I recognize a great danger in lifting up the rights revolution and the sexual revolution as vehicles for our ministry and our servanthood; but this accords with our biblical faith. If you were to ask me what is distinctive about the Christian faith, really distinctive of Christianity, I would reply that it would be the recognition that the divine disclosure occurs in our experience and our history. Moreover, that disclosure calls for a ministry and obedience in the midst of that history. In the personal sphere of sexuality and in the public sphere of rights, we are encountering authentic centers for a serious expression of our servanthood. These are the spheres of commitment opening before us.

4

A Christian Look at the
Sexual Revolution

•

PAUL LEHMANN

Differing both with the editor in Chapter 1 about whether there *is* a sexual revolution, and with Gibson Winter in Chapter 3 about the term's significance, Paul Lehmann turns our attention to the human search for sexual meaning. Writing from his stance in contextual ethics, he cites biblical tradition to de-emphasize the morality/immorality question and to emphasize the issue of human relations. Dr. Lehmann is professor of systematic theology at Union Theological Seminary in New York.

•

Reviewing a recent Off-Broadway preview, Mr. Clive Barnes remarked that the play "is rather like a string of soap operas stuck frothily together. . . . Very often it rings true. . . . A truism has to be true to be a truism." Mr. Barnes, then, went on to observe that "behind every cliché lies a thought not only promiscuous but also immortal." The play "is concerned with the holy state of matriarchy and suggests, rather pessimistically, that marriage is hell." Thus, in a substantive as well as in a semantic sense, the play, and Mr. Barnes's reflections upon it, bear directly upon our present concern.[1]

The word "revolution" which was first applied to the motions of the stars, and then acquired its proper and current application to politics, appears to be subject to another shift of meaning which makes it a convenient term for a motley assortment of referents.[2] "Revolution" has become a cliché; and never more surely than when it is applied to sexual behavior in the world at mid-twentieth century. To speak of "sexual revolution" does confuse the meaning of the word "revolution"; and it does so without commensurate illumination of our understanding of sexual behavior and its current problems. "Sex" or "sexual," moreover, are words which readily lend themselves to the mass media, with the result that sexuality receives almost profligate attention, becomes the focus of a style of life, and the assessment of what is really going on is correspondingly difficult.

It is, however, an intrinsic office of art to exhibit the point to which statistics point. And thus, a play, in which "the holy estate of matrimony" has become "the holy state of matriarchy" (in Mr. Barnes's phrase), and marriage is experienced not as heaven but

[1] See The New York Times, Thursday, 27 February 1969, p. 35. The play is by Allen Jack Lewis, and is called, A Corner of the Bed.
[2] Hannah Arendt, On Revolution, (New York: Viking Press, 1965) p. 35.

as hell, can bring to focus the confusion and variety in what is going on, and bid us take a sharp look at the situation and the emerging problems. "Behind every cliché lies a thought not only promiscuous but also immortal." Behind the semantic and sexual promiscuity of our time, an immortal thought is struggling to be born again. Being "born again" is, in turn, a central Christian passion and prospect. Consequently, it could be that a Christian look at the sexual revolution offers a way of bringing together two searching struggles to be born again, and in so doing, bringing "life and immortality to light." (2 Timothy 1:10)

Let us take up this offer by giving some attention to four aspects of it. They are: (1) The search for sexual meaning; (2) Why God made two sexes; (3) The mystery and threat of belonging; (4) The transfiguration of sexuality.

THE SEARCH FOR SEXUAL MEANING

As a human experience, sexuality is a relation of mystery and wonder, of fear and frustration, of freedom and fulfillment. The relation involves the fundamental mode of human differentiation and expresses the dynamics of dependence, independence, and interdependence which characterize man's growth into selfhood through the selfhood of another. The primordial name for this relation, to which language, myth and ritual assent, is the relation between male and female. Archetypal experiences, memories, and associations of a physical, and depth-psychological kind, with a concomitant sensitivity to mystery, seem to connect the word "sex" with the differentiation between male and female. Although the etymology is less than clear, at the root of the word, "sex," there seem to be the notions of "division" and "cutting." [3] Accordingly, it may be conjectured that these notions come by primordial associations to be connected with the fundamental human differentiation between male and female. The result is a semantic tautology

[3] To the Latin mind at any rate. So, *sexus* is referred by its users among the classical writers to *seco, secere, secui, sectus,* meaning "to cut." In Livy, we find the word *seco* used of a scratch or a wound, and of castration; in Ovid and Vergil, of making by cutting; in Cicero, of dividing.

which identifies "sex" with the relation between male and female; and the relation between male and female with "sex." But the semantic tautology is itself a sign of the human meaning of the sexual relation. Something more is going on in the differentiation between male and female than merely cellular division. What is going on is a dynamic reciprocity between vitality and meaning in the human search for identity and wholeness, between man as an animal and man who dreams dreams and sees visions of self-fulfillment in a community of freedom, love and trust, between man, driven by libidinal self-objectification back into his own self-satisfactions and man, released from narcissistic circularity by the polarity of a libidinal opposite. The dynamics of the sexual relation do indeed evoke the mystery and wonder of a freeing and fulfilling companionship and the fear and frustration of a threat of domination which castrates or brutalizes, according to the sexual reality of the other. ". . . The reason is," as Emil Brunner put it, almost a quarter century ago, "that the sex difference penetrates far more deeply than all individuality, and that the problem of sexuality is far more fundamental than that of individual characteristics. We cannot say that humanity is divided into the 'sanguine' and the 'choleric' temperament, into extroverts and introverts, into white or colored races, into geniuses and non-geniuses; but humanity certainly is divided into men and women, and this distinction goes to the very roots of our personal existence, and penetrates into the deepest 'metaphysical' grounds of our personality and our destiny." [4]

[4] Emil Brunner, *Man in Revolt.* (Philadelphia: Westminster Press, 1947), p. 345. Nor does the fact of homosexuality invalidate Brunner's point. If, as Helmut Thielecke has noted, homosexuality rests upon a latent mixture of the two sexes in one individual, it nevertheless points to the polarity of sexual differentiation. See H. Thielecke, *The Ethics of Sex.* (New York: Harper and Row, 1964), p. 3. It is important to keep the phenomenon of homosexuality always also in mind in the present discussion, not only because of what may be learned from it about heterosexual problems, but especially because of what homosexuality can tell us about the relation between creativity and human fulfillment. One thinks, for example, of the brilliant monograph by Hans Kelsen on *Platonic Love,* in *The American Image* (Boston, 1942). Kelsen tries to take seriously the possibility that Plato's understanding of love presupposes a homosexual spirituality and that Plato's pessimism about life in this

We have set out from these considerations because they deliver us from a persistent and widespread confusion about the sexual revolution. The sexual revolution tends to be alternately celebrated and condemned on moral grounds. Its proponents herald it as a moral advance, a bid for liberation, at long last, from confining social and ethical restrictions which deprive man of freedom and of the maturity which freedom takes. Those who view the sexual revolution with alarm tend to regard it as a bid for license in the name of liberty, as an exaltation of passion over reason, of uninhibited immediacy over restraint in the relations between male and female, and as the most obvious symptom of moral and social disintegration of our "sensate culture." [5] Those who hail the revolution seem to have sensed something of the mystery and wonder of sexuality, and in their excitement are wont to disregard the fear and frustration that belong to sexuality as culturally induced. Those who find themselves opposed to the change in the patterns of sexual behavior, against which they seem vainly trying to hold the line, find the fear and frustration that belong to sexuality so momentous and menacing as to deprive them of any serious attention to its mystery and wonder.

In the United States, at least, these rival estimates of the sexual revolution still ascribe their disagreement to the wisdom or unwisdom of Puritanism and/or to a companion mentality identified,

---

world, reinforced by the death of Socrates, was rooted in his having "experienced the tragic destiny of a one-sided homosexuality; and that just for this reason he necessarily entered into a deep and painful conflict with himself, with the world, and particularly with society." (Kelsen, p. 41). Even though we accept a daring characterization, like that of Warner Fite in *The Platonic Legend,* "that the Platonic spirituality is derived from pederasty" (quoted by Kelsen, p. 6), we are confronted the more strongly by the fundamental significance of the sexual relation for human fulfillment and by the enormous problem of the bisexual as compared to the heterosexual aspects of that relation. These considerations seem to point firmly toward the view that sexuality and its problems are fundamentally and primordially *human* in their mode and meaning and only secondarily and derivatively *moral,* if morality means the determination of what is right and wrong, good and bad, virtuous and vicious about the sexual relation.

[5] The phrase is Pitrim Sorokin's. See, P. Sorokin, *Society, Culture, and Personality,* New York, Harper and Row, 1947, p. 621ff.

especially in England, with her hapless Majesty, Victoria. But this seat of all our sexual troubles is being steadily disqualified by the impact of technology upon societies and cultures all around the world. In the wake of this impact, it appears that the ancient religions and cultures of the Far East are as sensitive to the fundamental character of sexual differentiation and to the dangers of sexual immediacy as Puritanism and Victorianism ever were. Meanwhile, the psycho-dynamics of sexuality, from Freud to Kinsey, have exhibited a range, diversity, inventiveness and intensity which leave the one-time citadels of sexual unease and restraint far behind and make "revolution" a quite proper word for rapidly changing patterns of sexual behavior. What makes these changes revolutionary, however, is not alone their rate and range. More important is the increasingly inescapable impression of a certain frenzied insistence that a wholly new order of sexual behavior is called for, with a corresponding alteration of sexual values. In so far as these values do not merely substitute freedom for restraint, frankness for diffidence, experimentation for prohibition, they seem to exhibit a curious paradox. There is a search for sexual meaning going on which, on the one hand, seems quite ready to jettison the time-honored relation between sex, love, and marriage while, on the other hand, insisting upon integrity in sexual relations as the presupposition of the human meaning of sexuality which has been the fundamental point of the wisdom of the race as regards sexual experience and practice. This means that old values are being "repackaged," not basically and brashly being repudiated. Thus, the sexual revolution is poised, as it were, on the frontier between the rejection of the sexual experience and wisdom of the past and the reshaping of that experience and wisdom, at the level both of practice and of meaning.

A little more than two decades have passed since the controversial Kinsey reports gave documentary notice of a sexual revolution in the making.[6] The distance between these studies and two

---

[6] Alfred C. Kinsey, *Sexual Behavior in the Human Male*, Philadelphia, W.B. Saunders Co., 1948; and its sequel: *Sexual Behavior in the Human Female*, Philadelphia, W.B. Saunders Co., 1953.

recently published responses to the rate and range of changing sexual patterns measures more than accumulating statistical confirmation of Kinsey's findings.[7] What is being measured is the increasing urgency of a perspective with power to give shape and direction to sexual understanding and experience. It could be that the sexual revolution has turned a corner and that what is now called for is not so much more information about what is going on as more information about the "kind of insights desperately needed by anyone trying to understand what has happened to the old morality and to relate creatively to persons groping about for guidance in the midst of the sexual wilderness." [8]

Our thesis, then, may be formulated in a threefold way. The thesis is: *1) that the sexual revolution of our time, in its wildest as well as in its quiet forms, is fundamentally a search for sexual meaning; 2) that this search exhibits a sensitivity to the fundamental relation between humanity and sexuality in the life of man; and 3) that when we shift our attention from the morality or immorality of sexual behavior to the human factor in the basic relations between male and female, we begin to move across the frontier between the rejection and the reshaping of the sexual experience and wisdom of the past, and to come in sight of the possibility of joining freedom with responsibility in sexual experience and practice.*

It should be emphasized that in putting the matter in this way, we do not mean to dissociate sexuality from morality. Nor do we overlook the important connection between morality and human-

[7] See, for example, Brooks R. Walker, *The New Immorality: A Report on Spouse-Trading, Pornography, Playboy Philosophy, and Situation Ethics*, New York, Doubleday, 1968; and Vance Packard, *The Sexual Wilderness: The Contemporary Upheaval in Male-Female Relationships*, New York, McKay, 1968. The titles confirm in a vivid way the revolutionary character of sexual behavior, the fundamental relation involved in this behavior, the current confusion about the meaning and practice of sexual experience, and the mounting intensity of the search for sexual meaning. The descriptive literature is so voluminous as to make the present volume a timely attempt to shift the focus of attention from description to interpretation.

[8] Harry E. Smith, in a review article entitled *The Sexual Revolution*, in *The Christian Century*, Volume LXXXVI, No. 2, January 8, 1969, p. 52.

ity in the life and behavior of man. What we wish to suggest is
that although the search for meaning intrinsically includes the
search for values, and thus involves moral insights and the making
of moral judgments, these values, insights and judgments are the
hard-won gains, not the norms, of sexual experience and practice.
They function as guidelines which each generation must confirm
for itself, not as superimposable patterns of sexual behavior. And
they are as *good* and as "useful" as their discoverable power to
make room for what is fundamentally and fulfillingly human in
sexual relations.

These relations between humanity, sexuality and morality are
instructively illuminated by the current debate over the Swedish
film, *I Am Curious (Yellow)*.[9] Although I have not seen the film,
a basic question apparently raised by it is whether the relation
between sexuality and humanity can be rediscovered through the
conjunction of morality and art. The direct filming of the sexual
act by exposing to view two human bodies, one male, the other
female, in the concrete and intimate meeting through which love
ministers to human identity and wholeness, seems to be trying to
face without subterfuge the critical instance of the bond between
sexuality and humanity. In so doing, sexual experience and understanding are being transposed from one level of morality to another. The constrictive confinements with which taboo and custom, social, legal, moral, and religious prohibition and negation
have enveloped sexual experience and behavior are being shifted to
another level of moral sensitivity and possibility. On this level, the
sexual act is the sign that two people on the search for the identity of each, have found the identity of each in the other by moving through bodily union beyond the basic separateness of each,
toward the fulfillment of each in the other. What art contributes
to morality is a vision of human sensitivity and promise in which

---

[9] See, for example, the discussion by John Simon, "Getting Curious Over
Curious," in the drama section of *The New York Times* of Sunday, 9 February
1969; and the discussion in *Look* by its European Editor, Leonard Gross,
"After Nudity, What, Indeed?' (Vol. 33, #9, 29 April 1969), pp. 80-82.
Walter Kerr has also discussed the film in *The New York Times* of 2 Febru-
ary 1969.

the animalic, the gross, the chaotic, the brutal, the Dionysian fury, have been displaced by the grace, the delicateness, the delight, the power and beauty of form in formation. "Form," as Ben Shahn has noted, "is the very shape of content." [10] On the other hand, what morality contributes to art is a vision of human integrity and wholeness, of the limits within which freedom makes fulfillment possible, of responsiveness which takes responsibility for freedom, of the commitments and fidelities which make the risks of freedom and the prospects of fulfillment plausible. Whether or not *I Am Curious (Yellow)* achieves its purposed conjunction of morality and art, at the level of art, appears indeed to be debatable. It can, however, be said that the degree to which the film fails as an artistic achievement is the degree to which it also fails as a moral achievement. When the artistic vision blurs, or is betrayed, the moral vision disintegrates and morality becomes the enemy of man. Whether or not *I Am Curious (Yellow)* is to be judged pornographic or prurient, Dionysian or dull, tantalizing or tedious, in short, immoral or inane depends upon the clarity and constancy of its artistic and moral vision. Failure here would mean that once again the bond between sexuality and humanity has been violated, and one more immoral attack upon the morality and immorality of sexual behavior has been loosed upon a sexually confused and wayward society. The film would, then, have joined *Playboy* in the dehumanization of sexuality through a moralistic protest against the moralization of sex. Achievement here, however, would mean that the search for sexual meaning had moved "beyond good and evil," right and wrong, and come in sight of an humanizing possibility for sexual freedom and responsibility. The filming of the sexual act signals the search for sexual meaning in search of its "moment of truth" in the bond between sexuality and humanity.

WHY GOD MADE TWO SEXES

The late Helen Hokinson, who for many years delighted readers of *The New Yorker* with her cartoon sketches of amiable, matronly

[10] Ben Shahn, *The Shape of Content.* (Cambridge: Harvard University Press, 1957), p. 53.

dowagers, once depicted two of these in conversation. Said one of them to the other, "I just love the idea of there being two sexes!" So also does God the Almighty Creator, Maker of heaven and earth!

The "moment of truth" in the search for sexual meaning is anchored in creation. As the very first chapter of Genesis so beautifully puts its: "God said, 'Let us make man in our image, in the likeness of ourselves, and let them be masters of the fish of the sea, the birds of heaven, the cattle, all wild beasts, and all the reptiles that crawl upon the face of the earth.'

> God created man in the image of himself,
> in the image of himself God he created him,
> male and female he created them.

God blessed them, saying to them, "Be fruitful, multiply, fill the earth and conquer it." [11] Clearly, both the productive and the reproductive experience of man with "the face of the earth" underlies this assessment of basics and beginnings. It is also clear, though not as steadily kept in mind, that these basics and beginnings are purposed. They involve an originating and a sovereign calling into being for a fulfilling destiny. Creation means purposed beginnings, foundations for fulfillment *of* the world as experienced and *in* the world as experienced. Between foundations and fulfillment, beginnings and destiny, there lies the vast matrix of differentiating occasions and the wide horizon of promise and possibility which mark the givenness of things and the sign and seal of meaning and of creativity. When the world is received as gift and participation in it as an opportunity, the world is experienced as creation. As creation, the world is experienced as taking form from beyond itself and running out toward a consummation beyond itself, and the shape of things between is the sign of the shape of things to come. According to the Bible, the word "God," which we use so easily and emptily, functions as a title. Actually, the title presupposes a long familiarity with another way of identifying the

[11] Genesis 1:26-27; as given in the Jerusalem Bible. This version will be used throughout this chapter, unless otherwise noted.

Giver of the given, the Creator of creation. If we remember that the word "God" refers to the one whom the Bible calls, "Lord" and "Father," the word becomes both useful and clear. Otherwise, the word is understandably and rightly expendable.[12]

So, God, as the Bible understands the word, is the "Lord" who creates, sustains, and fulfills the world and all things in it. He sets the boundaries, the limits within which all things are called to be what they are, and to enjoy the freedom to discover *that* they are and *what* they are through responsive participation in the purposes of purposed life. If Genesis is right, there is one momentous, though not total exception, among the creatures in God's creation. He is *the Creature*, as Karl Barth has strikingly put it.[13] He is *the* Creature in the sense that he shares with all creatures the purposed givenness of life in the world and the enjoyment of the freedom to discover *that* and *what* they are. Unlike all other creatures, however, *the Creature* who bears the name, *Man,* (Hebrew: *Adam*) is called to mastery and is marked by a unique identity. This identity involves a radical shift of pronouns occasioned by the gift in creaturehood of an identifying companionship. The enjoyment of the freedom to discover *that* and *what* man is, is exercised in the enjoyment of the freedom to discover *who* he is. In the mystery and wonder of this *who-ness*, man experiences the gift of his likeness to God and of selfhood through his radically opposite number. Man is who he is in the relation of male and female and this is his likeness to God. Thus, sexual differentiation is the basic mode of "who-ness"; and sexuality becomes the bearer of identity. When this relation is "in order," that is, when the sexual relation functions as the gift of the freedom to be who one is in the fulfilling companionship of a radically different other, celebration and creation characterize man's mastery over all creation. "The book," says Sister Corita, "talks about man being made

[12] I owe this suggestion to Professor Helmut Gollwitzer's fourth Hewitt lecture on *Who Is "God" in The Story of Reconciliation*, Union Theological Seminary, 1968. Unpublished.

[13] Karl Barth, *Church Dogmatics*, (New York: Charles Scribner's Sons.) (Edinburgh: T. and T. Clark) Vol. III/2, 1960; p. 4.

                in the image and likeness
                        of god
                in the context of the creation story
        and we get the idea that man is called to be like god
                                as creator
                                as maker
        in a sense every man is supposed to be an artist . . .
        art is the work of a person
                        a human being
                who is free to take into himself what he sees outside
                        and from his free center
                                put his human stamp on it
        the artist is the sign to the whole world
                that reality
                        or the world
                        is shaped by man
                                and not the other way around . . .
        one way to prepare for big celebrations
                is to allow life to reveal its many small ones
                        to keep it from being so daily
        there are three things that keep life
                from being so daily
                        to make love
                        to make believe
                                to make hope
                with
        the ordinary everyday people and stuff
                                around us [14]"

Sister Corita's lines about creation and art are about man. Her
lines about celebration concern, in her own boldly chosen type,
GOD! What happens to sex in man's activity of creation and
celebration? Perhaps, there is a hint of an answer in the consideration that *I Am Curious (Yellow)* is a "headline" to which Sister

[14] Sister Corita, *Footnotes and Headlines.* (New York: Herder and Herder,
1967), pp. 20, 21, 23, 16.

Corita's celebration and creation is a "footnote." The "headline" is a statement about the identity of man. The "footnote" is a statement about the man who is free in his identity for celebration and creation. The man who is free in this way is "male and female." And this is the man by whom "the whole world . . . is shaped and not the other way around." "Not the other way around"—both in Sister Corita's sense that the world does not shape man but man shapes the world; and in the sense of the film that without the freedom to be who he is, man cannot participate in celebration and creation. Thus, God made man male and female so that they might "be masters of the fish of the sea, the birds of heaven, the cattle, all wild beasts, and all the reptiles that crawl upon the face of the earth," and in this mastery enjoy the mystery and wonder of their identity. The conjunction of man's mastery of the earth with the mystery and wonder of his identity preserves each from the idolatry to which each without the other is prone. Mastery without mystery despoils the earth which it has conquered because dominion has become domination. Mystery without mastery is despoiled of the wonder of identity because Narcissus has usurped the gift of the image of God to man as male and female, and each becomes the bearer to the other, not of the selfhood of the other but of its own. Apollo and Dionysius are, as Norman O. Brown has rightly shown, immortally mortal enemies. But at the root of the enmity is not, as Brown seems to suggest, the suppression of Dionysian vitality owing to the default of Christianity upon its commitment to the resurrection of the body (this Christianity has also done) and the alliance of Christian and Apollonian exaltations of the formative power of thought (*logos? idos?*), but rather the titanism by which Apollonian and Dionysian power have "exchanged the glory of the immortal God for a worthless imitation, *for the image* of mortal man, of birds, of quadrupeds and reptiles." [15] The self-image of the creature has usurped the image of

[15] See Romans 1:23; Jerusalem Bible, to which the italics also refer. See also Norman O. Brown, *Life Against Death*. (New York: Vintage Books, 1959). Mr. Brown's Freudian reading of history is imaginative, incisive and illuminating, especially as regards the relation between sexuality and creativity.

God the creator. *Eritis sicut Deus!*

The strange reciprocity between the search for sexual meaning and the Genesis account of the place and importance of sexuality in the creaturehood of man, "made in the image of God," should prepare a Christian to look at the sexual revolution of our time with less surprise and considerably more understanding than is widely the case. The stereotypes are that the church is a major and long-time bulwark of sexual repression and rigid codes of sexual behavior and that sexual meaning begins with the repudiation of the teaching, and increasingly of the fellowship, of the church and the pursuit, instead, of uninhibited sexual satisfactions. Indeed, the "double portion" of ignominy which has been heaped upon Queen Victoria in this matter is due in so small degree to her own Christian piety. How is it that the Christian interpretation of sexuality has taken a turn which seems so greatly at variance with the basics and beginnings set out in the book of Genesis? Surely the church in faithfulness to Holy Scripture should have come into a quite opposite public image. Instead of being a leader in the rearguard of sexual conservatism, the church belongs to her biblical charter in the vanguard of sexual freedom. This is scarely the occasion for a review of the history of the matter. Yet it is germane to recall that more than a blind and stubborn piety or a flagrant disregard of the plain teaching of Scripture is involved.

For one thing, it is hazardous to rest the whole case for a positive and liberating Christian view of sexuality and sexual behavior upon the biblical account of the image of God. It is well known that the passages in the Bible which expressly mention the image of God are few in number.[16] These are mainly in the book of

---

But his celebration of Dionysian over Apollonian cultural and behavorial themes and motifs seems to take insufficient account of the relation between the mystery and wonder of identity and man's mastery of the world he is to shape. Consequently, the resurrection of the body becomes a rhythmic pattern of cultural death and life and not the resurrection of the body made in the image of God for life everlasting. Brown's fascinating shift of accent is at best a Christian variant of resurrection faith, at least, a gnostic deviant. See especially Chapter XII.

[16] Expressly Gen. 1:26-27; 5:1,3; 9:6; James 3:9. Indirectly, Ps. 8:5-6; Col. 3:10; Ro. 1:23-4.

Genesis. As for the New Testament, the image of God is used as a description of Jesus Christ; and men are said to be renewed in the image of Christ.[17] Moreover, as the biblical story moves beyond the accounts of creation, the attention shifts markedly to God's dealings with the people whom he has chosen in covenant, to deliverance and fulfillment of their history and destiny. Where man is up for attention, the focus of concern is with his disobedience and sin, with the conflict between flesh and spirit, and with grace and salvation. Not only are the relations between sexuality and the image of God largely overtaken by these other motifs of biblical faith and story; but sexuality tends to be subsumed under the taboo and customs of tribal and nomadic society and both guarded and guided by the seventh commandment, and Jesus' reaffirmation and intensification of it. "You have learnt how it was said," he declared, "*you must not commit adultery*. But I say this to you: if a man looks at a woman lustfully, he has already committed adultery with her in his heart." [18] At stake here is the displacement of the mystery and wonder of sexuality by fear and frustration owing to the operational loss of man's unique and creative relation to God. The will to freedom in obedience has succumbed to the will to power, owing to a radical depravation, experienced as nothing less than as a "fall," a fall from the grace of creation.[19] The "take-over" of sexuality by the commandment

17 Ro. 8:29; 1 Cor. 11:7; 2 Cor. 3:18,4:4; Col. 1:5,3:10.

18 Matthew 5:27. The seventh commandment reads: "You must not commit adultery." It may be found in Ex. 20:14; and Dt. 5:18.

19 It must be noted that Catholic and Reformation theology differ sharply over the question of the effect of the Fall upon the image of God. Catholic theology speaks of a corruption of the image of God, occasioned by sin but not of a total destruction of it. There are *reliquies imaginis Dei*, remnants of the image of God in human nature, which are the basis of man's continuing sensitivity to the claims of God and the starting points for his renewal in that image. Reformation theology accents *total depravity*—not in the sense that the image of God has been totally destroyed by the Fall, but in the sense that the image has been rendered operationally useless. It cannot serve as the basis of human renewal, or even of man's continuing sensitivity to the claims of God. Only as this sensitivity and this renewal are radically transformed by the relation of man to Christ who, in a world of sin, *is* the image of God, can and does man's loss of his unique identity give way before its restoration as a

has tended to obscure the original and fundamental relation of sexuality to humanity, and to emphasize prohibition of sexual behavior over participation in it.

If one were to single out any individuals, as the conceptual architects of such a "take-over," the assignment would go to Paul of Tarsus and Augustine of Hippo. It has been judiciously remarked that "no impartial assessment, . . . can ignore in St. Paul's attitude to sexual matters an ascetical bias which, though it stops short of dualism, accords but a grudging recognition to marriage, and exalts virginity as a religious ideal. . . . The eschatological context of the Apostle's words was forgotten, and matrimony was set forth as a way of life, permitted indeed by God and possessing a certain positive value, but intrinsically and in all circumstances less perfect than singleness . . ." [20] As for Augustine, he drew upon St. Paul in his attempt to transcend his own struggles in the warfare of passion with spirit, identified sexuality as the source and center of that struggle, and went further than any Christian thinker in connecting human sexuality with the Fall.[21] The greater the distance between any given contemporary attitude toward sexual behavior and the New Testament and early Church, the harder it is also to remember that, in his own time, Paul's views on sexuality and marriage would have seemed reasonable enough to most of his contemporaries. In their eyes, he was trying to find a way

---

free gift. By the same token, the frustration and fear which prevent the mystery and wonder of sexuality from issuing in sexual freedom and fulfillment cannot and are not broken through and left behind except as the relation of male and female is set free by the relation of each to the reconciling presence and power of Jesus Christ in the world.

[20] Derrick S. Bailey, *Sexual Relation in Christian Thought*, New York, Harper and Brothers, 1959, p. 14. The author suggests that here lay "the germ of a new double ethical standard" at once damaging and profound in its influence upon Christian conceptions of spirituality and sexuality. The book is a reliable and instructive account of the history of Christian thought about sexual matters.

[21] D.S. Bailey, *Ibid.*, pp. 52ff. Augustine tells us in his Confessions (VIII, xii, 30), how agonized he had been upon reading Paul's admonition against making "provision for the flesh, to fulfill the lusts thereof" (Ro. 13:13-14), and how he had come gradually to exalt continence as the mark of obedience to his conversion.

between the "naturalism typical of his Jewish heritage" and "the pessimistic dualism of Hellenistic philosophy." [22] Augustine likewise found himself contemporary with the declining decades of a great world civilization, and, possessed as he was, with a restless and gifted mind and spirit, he found himself not unnaturally led to ponder the shuddering contrast between "Paradise Then" and "Paradise Now." He could not find in the *freedom over* inhibitions of "Paradise Now" a recovery of the *freedom from* inhibitions of "Paradise Then." In the original Paradise, according to Augustine, Adam and Eve were "naked and unashamed because their genitals, like their other members, were wholly under control and obedient to the dictates of the will . . . They did not venture upon coitus before their expulsion from Eden, but had they done so, their congress would have been without lascivious heat or unseemly passion. . . . But when pride and self-will led the pair into sin, a new experience befell them . . . , they became conscious within themselves of a new and destructive impulse, . . . by which they were driven to an insatiable quest for self-satisfaction." [23] Augustine called this inordinate desire, *concupiscence.* He noted, in the declining civilization all about him, abundant evidence of the immediate satisfaction of inordinate desire, and sought to hold before his contemporaries another vision of human identity and fulfillment. According to that vision, the love of God is the secret of self-hood and the source of true and fulfilling desire.

Succeeding generations, however, exhibit exceedingly short memories. Consequently, the Augustinian syndrome binding inordinate desire to sexuality and sexuality to sin functioned as an increasingly restrictive confinement to their past of generations yet unborn. It mattered less and less that in *their* day, Paul and Augustine profoundly glimpsed the complexity and depth of the relation between sexuality and humanity and underlined the ambiguity and the difficulty of the search for sexual meaning. What has come down across the centuries to us *in our day* is a deep and dark suspicion

[22] D.S. Bailey, *Ibid.*, pp. 12,13.
[23] D.S. Bailey, *Ibid.*, pp. 53-54. The reader may find in the notes to these pages, the documentation from Augustine himself.

of sexuality and a corresponding loss of sensitivity to the peril as well as to the promise of the original and fundamental link between sexuality and the humanity of man. As regards sensitivity to the peril and the promise of the sexual relation, Jesus shared the tradition which had been anchored in the Old Testament and had shaped the Judaism of his day. His strictures against adultery and divorce express no negative view of the sexual relation. On the contrary, they intensify the high and healthy view of the relation of sexuality to the family and of the profound connection between monogamy and monotheism to which the covenant relation between Yahweh and the people whom he had chosen for his own had given rise.[24] Indeed, the paradigm of the freedom and fidelity which mark the stability and the integrity of Jewish attitudes toward marriage and the family is the freedom and fidelity of God's purposed faithfulness toward his people and their destiny. Thus, *more basic to Christianity than the Augustinian syndrome, binding inordinate desire to sexuality and sexuality to sin, is the monotheism: monogamy syndrome which informed Jesus' heritage and his own view of sexual meaning and fulfillment.* This latter syndrome is the operational outcome of the original and originating relation between God and man, as Creator and unique creature, a relation in which the union and communion of male and female is the concrete and human meaning of the image of God.[25] A Christian look at the sexual revolution begins from this point. It finds here a perspective from which to understand *that* and *why*

[24] Or at least between henotheism and monogamy. We need not enter here upon the historical problem whether and in how far Israel's faith and life were shaped by the belief in *one God alone* (monotheism) or in *only one God* (henotheism). It seems to us that the first commandment, which excludes all other Gods but Yahweh (Ex. 20:1-2) is functional monotheism; and that this monotheism may be regarded as a formative and sustaining factor—if not a foundational one—in the stability and the humanizing role of the family in Jewish life. See N. P. Williams, *The Ideas of the Fall and Original Sin.* (London, 1927) Lectures I and II; D.S. Bailey, *op. cit.*, chapter 1.

[25] So far as I am aware, Karl Barth is the first major theologian of the church to read the *image of God* in this way, and in so doing, to offer the possibility of breaking out of the Augustinian syndrome. See Barth, *op. cit.*, especially Par. 45, 3, pp. 291-2, 301-16. See also, C.D., III/1, Par. 41, 2, pp. 288ff.

God made two sexes. The reason is that the relation between male and female is the concrete bearer of the secret of human identity, freedom and fulfillment. In the sexual relation, man receives and knows who he is as a gift, and in the freedom of this selfhood discovers in every creaturely relation an occasion for his own creativity and wholeness.

The Mystery and Threat of Belonging

If a Christian look at the sexual revolution starts from a perspective indicated by the *image of God,* a Christian cannot look at the sexual revolution very long without becoming aware of an almost devastating problem. The problem is that the search for sexual meaning and God's reason for making two sexes seem to cancel each other out. Why, it must be asked, has the dynamics of the search for sexual meaning acquired revolutionary proportions if sexuality is and functions as the behavioral sign of the unique creatureliness of man? To insist upon looking at the sexual revolution from this perspective is to succumb to the dilemma, on the one hand, of looking away from what is really going on (abstractness), or, on the other hand, of really looking into what is going on only to discover that Christianity has nothing significant to say about it (irrelevance). The sexual revolution is one more sign, even though a particularly poignant and regrettable one, that Christianity is hopelessly caught between abstraction and irrelevance, and has been overtaken by events. The present attempt likewise is foredoomed by this dilemma, having taken a conspicuously circuitous route from "Paradise Then" to "Paradise Now." At this point in our discussion, we seem to have left "where it's sexually at" far behind, and to be playing a familiar theological ostrich game.

Perhaps so. Perhaps we are engaged in the theological game of shoring up the Bible as an "authority-book," Jesus as an "authority-figure," and an obsolescent Christianity as a viable life-style. To this, at least two replies may be made. One is, candidly to admit the possibility. Christianity is intrinsically extrinsic. That is, it confronts man in his world with the reality of a radically originative and renewing option, as a claim to which there can be but a single response. When the response is made, what began with a pressure from without is experienced as a freedom from within. Should there be no response, the pressure from without can only be regarded as an "authority" which prevents authentic freedom from within. In addition, the case for Christianity can always be inadequately or erroneously made. The other reply to the question whether a theological game is being played is an apostolic one. It recalls a similar predicament of Paul of Tarsus. In that wild and dissolute town of Corinth, he had once organized a group of Christians into a congregation. They were a contentious group, and once raised with him the question of the ostrich game. Paul wrote back as follows:

> And so it is with the fear of the Lord in mind that we try to win people over. God knows us for what we really are, and I hope that in your consciences you know us too. This is not another attempt to commend ourselves to you: we are simply giving you reasons . . . so that you will have an answer ready for the people who can boast *more about what they seem than what they are.* If we seemed out of our senses, it was for God; but if we are being reasonable now, it is for your sake. . . . Corinthians, we have spoken to you very frankly; our mind has been opened in front of you. Any constraint that you feel is not on our side; the constraint is in your own selves. I speak as if to children of mine: as a fair exchange, open your minds in the same way.[26]

Suppose, then, that we take into account the possibility of such "a fair exchange," and open our minds "in the same way." In so doing, it will be apparent that we have not been taking the long way around at all. Actually, we have been converging upon the crucial point of intersection between the search for sexual meaning and the perspective from which a Christian is directed by his faith to look at the sexual revolution now in process. This point is the deep and concrete experience of the mystery and the threat of belonging. In its depths, and in the last analysis, the search for

---

[26] II Corinthians 5:11-12; 6:11-13a. Italics mine.

sexual meaning is the search for a relation of fundamental, dependable and liberating belonging, a relation in which freedom and fidelity accompany the gift of identity, that is, of self-accepting selfhood. In its depths, and in the last analysis, the Christian assessment of the bond between sexuality and humanity focuses upon, and is derived from precisely such a relation. As Karl Barth has put it:

". . . the account of the creation of man as male and female is the climax of the whole history of creation. . . . In this . . . there is a radical rejection of isolation. And the point of the whole text is to say and tell . . . who and what is the man who is created good by God . . . This man . . . must have a partner like himself, and must therefore be a partner to a being like himself; to a being in which he can recognize himself, and yet not himself but another, seeing it is not only like him but also different from him; in other words, a 'help meet.' This helpmeet is woman. . . . God the Creator knows and ordains, but He leaves it to man to discover, that only woman and not animals can be this helpmeet. Thus the climax of the history of creation coincides with this *first act of human freedom*. . . . In the first instance, (man) exercises his human freedom, his humanity, negatively. He remains free for the being which the Creator will give him as a partner. He waits for woman and can do so. *He must not grasp after a false completion*. But who and what is woman? She is not (man's) postulate, or ideal, let alone his creation. Like himself, she is the thought and work of God. . . . *She is not merely there to be arbitrarily and accidentally discovered and accepted by man*. As God creates both man and woman, He also creates their relationship and brings them together. But this divinely created relationship—which is not just any kind of relationship, but the distinctive human relationship—has to be recognized and affirmed by man himself. . . . Here we have *the second and positive step in the act of freedom*, in the venture of thought and speech, of man exercising his humanity in this freedom. *At the heart of his humanity he is free in and for the fact that he may recognize and accept the woman whom he himself has not imagined and conjured up by his desire, but whom God has created and brought*. With this choice he confirms who and what he is within creation, . . . the particularity of his creation. . . . *Human being becomes the being in encounter in which alone it can be good.* . . . 'Therefore shall a man leave his father and his mother, and shall cleave unto his wife' means that because woman is so utterly *from* man he must be utterly *to* her, because she is so utterly for him he must be utterly for her; because she can only follow him in order that he should not be alone he must also follow her not to be alone; because he the first and stronger can only be one and strong in relationship to her he must accept and treat her, the second and weaker, as his first and stronger. *It is in this inversion that the possibility of the human,* the natural supremacy of the I over the Thou, *is developed in reality.* It is in this way that the genuinely human declares its possibility. . . . *The human is the male and female in its differentiation but also its connexion."* [27]

This passage puts so precisely what the search for sexual meaning is all about, and what its source and sum and secret are, that we have ventured to include it at some length. It can only be urged that before following the present account of a Christian look at the sexual revolution to its close, Barth's words be pondered with all possible reflective care. They say exactly what the mystery of belonging is. It is the mystery wherein and whereby the sexual relation between male and female is the basis and the bearer of the self-identity of man, and of the freedom and fidelity to be human in the world. The identity-freedom-fidelity syndrome defines the structure and the dynamics of belonging and exhibits the intimacy and the ultimacy of the bond between sexuality and humanity.

Belonging is the experience of a relation through which man knows who he is, as and where he is, in what he does. What he does is responds, from a center of unified and stable selfhood, in a free act of self-giving to another self, similarly centered, unified and stable. Belonging is being with and for another, through whom the gift of identifiable selfhood has come, *freely,* that is, without dissimulation and self-justification. Belonging is the experience of receiving yourself, as and where you are, as a gift from another who has similarly received you, and finding in everything around you,

[27] Karl Barth, *Church Dogmatics,* Vol. III/2, pp. 291-92. Italics and parentheses mine.

so many different ways of saying, "Thank you." Thus, belonging is the human and humanizing presupposition and power of involvement. And this is why sexuality is fundamental to human fulfillment.

Long before the epoch-making Freudian discovery and documentation of the dynamics of selfhood, Christian faith had been put by its biblical basis and perspectives upon the track of what Freud had explored with consummate precision and care. However persuasively post-Freudian corrections of the master's overextended concentration upon the role of sexuality in personality may have been established, it is still notable that Freud and the Bible are in agreement about the sexual basics and beginnings of the freedom and wholeness of man as a person, that is, of what being human means. Just as "man does not live on bread alone, but on every word that comes from the mouth of God," so man does not live on sex alone but on every word that illuminates the human meaning of his life from birth to death, and of his insistent hopes and visions of life beyond death.[28] Man does, however, also live on bread; so also, he lives on sex. And just as life on bread, apart from the "bread of life," is left to itself, becomes a destructive occasion of idolatrous conflict, so also, life on sex, apart from its Eucharistic nourishment, becomes a "battle of the sexes" in the course of which, each dehumanizes the other. The mystery of belonging is sustained and renewed by the presence of Christ against the threat of belonging. This is why in the Catholic Church, marriage is a sacrament, and a nuptial mass its proper celebration. This is also why it is regrettable that in the Catholic Church Reformed, a proper faithfulness to Jesus' indications of his sacramental presence has rightly insisted upon marriage as a holy ordinance rather than a sacrament but has wrongly divorced the celebration of marriage from its Eucharistic culmination. A wedding is simply a romantic disregard of the human fact that sexuality aims at belonging, that belonging involves threat as well as mystery, and that marriage is a sign that the bond between sexuality and humanity

[28] So Jesus quotes Deuteronomy 8:3 in Matthew's account of his temptation (4:4).

must again and again be forged anew in and by the presence of Christ.

The threat of belonging is the libidinal domination of the self by the other. It means that the mystery and wonder of the sexual relation has come under the ominous shadow of frustration and fear. The structure of belonging, according to which the identity-freedom-fidelity syndrome expresses and sustains the experience and power of selfhood has become a syndrome without sustaining structure, a syndrome of anonymity, diversion and mistrust, which transmutes the other from the bearer of selfhood into the enemy who enslaves and ultimately destroys the self. The pathos of the search for sexual meaning which characterizes the sexual revolution of our time is that it is a search for a sustaining structure of belonging which has both abandoned and been deprived of the perspective and power by which the purposed basics of sexual experience and behavior nourish sensitivity to what it takes to keep the threat of belonging from destroying the mystery and wonder of it.

This pathos pervades every level of sexual behavior. The high school or college adolescent, making his initial and intermittent discoveries of the pleasure and fascination of participation in the physical and emotional responsiveness of the sexually other, finds himself caught between what used to be called ecstasy and shame but, with the increasing distance between the sexual and the human in sexual experience, has come to be taken for granted as a private satisfaction with the self-evidence that goes with "being with it." A few weeks ago, The New York Times Magazine carried an extended account of upper-class, and particularly graduate students, who are eschewing marriage while living together, endeavoring in this way to find sexual and human fulfillment without making ultimate commitments prematurely, and in the quiet hope that growing together sexually and humanly will be more promising under the freedom to abandon the relation without reciprocal hurt and without the costs and complications involved in divorce.[29]

[29] Karlen Arno, "The Unmarried Marrieds on Campus," The New York Times Magazine, January 26, 1969.

Spouse-swapping, with or without the formalities of divorce, is a sufficiently discernible pattern of life in suburbia to notice that the practice is no respecter of baptismal covenants or of the responsibilities of church membership or of family and community status, with or without church connections. The question posed by the practice is whether the dubious reciprocity between ennui and excitement is a tolerably satisfying alternative to a marriage relationship which has steadily declined in sexual and human meaning. The generation gap which is more and more evidently a basic difference of life-style than of age has found in the sexual revolution a basic similarity beneath and beyond its variegated ritualizations. When parents of teen-aged youth, or of youth in early adulthood are unable to share a wisdom born of their own participation in the structure of belonging because they are caught up in "sexual affairs" of their own, age and youth would seem to have been joined in a poignant companionship occasioned by the surrender of the mystery and wonder of belonging to the threat of it.

Here we may return to the possible artistic and moral failure of *I Am Curious, (Yellow)*. If there is a failure, it may be ascribed not to Mr. Vilgot Sjoeman, the director's refusal to propose a solution to the search for sexual meaning. The search means that the sexual revolution has not yet arrived at a resolution of its quest. The artistic and moral failure of the film lies in its failure to exhibit the ambiguity between the mystery and the threat of belonging which pervades the search for sexual meaning. Lena's sexual fantasies, rooted in an almost wildly promiscuous search for a lover with whom she could enter into the structure of belonging is incongruous with her involvement in Swedish political life. The grim ending which finds both her and her lover in a completely functional VD clinic in Sweden's anxiety-free Socialist Commonwealth, detaches the agony of the threat of belonging from the search for sexual meaning and dehumanizes the wonder of belonging through the self-evidence of technical solutions which have disposed of the humanizing suffering occasioned by the sexual experience of ecstasy and shame. If *Look*'s editor [30] is correct that

[30] Leonard Gross, in *Look, op. cit.*, p. 82.

Miss Nyman (Lena) and Mr. Sjoeman "both want . . . an environment in which neither suppression nor rebellion would distort individual choice," they cannot rest the case upon the cliché that "lack of commitment in affairs of state is as disastrous as in affairs of heart." They have been careless of Mr. Barnes's insight from which we set out in this discussion, and have lost the "immortal thought" behind the cliché. This thought is that the basic bond between sexuality and humanity is purposed in the structure of belonging, and that the ambiguity between the mystery and the threat of belonging is a sign that, in the depth of the struggle to belong, the search for sexual meaning has crossed a frontier and become a concrete and very human search for an humanizing faith. Mere protest against moralization in the name of "an environment in which neither suppression nor rebellion would distort individual choice" is a trivialization of the human meaning of sexuality. Thus, it becomes a moralization of its own, and shows that moralization, whether in the church or at the cinema, undermines the possibility of joining freedom with responsibility in sexual experience and behavior.

How vastly different, in the integrity of sensitivity to this possibility, is the steady stream of sardonic commentary provided by Steig and Steinberg in the pages of *The New Yorker*.[31] They seem to be carrying forward the work of James Thurber, who once published a pictorial statement of one of his major themes, under the title, "Men, Women, and Dogs," with a subtitle, "The Battle of the Sexes." [32] In Mr. Thurber's view, the threat of belonging is so

[31] One thinks at random of Mr. Steinberg's Cover Caricature (Vol. XLIV, No. 40, 23 November 1968) and of Mr. Steig's caricature (Vol. XLV, No. 4, 15 March 1969, p. 138). The former depicts a dominant and domineering head of the family whose libidinal repressions have been transmitted to his son. Both father and son appear to have deprived their wives so completely of the freedom to be themselves as to give them the appearance of a mere replica of the human identity they once possessed. Meanwhile, both father and son substitute for this identity the fantasies of sensuous mistresses. Mr. Steig's piece takes the opposite tack and depicts a dominant and domineering wife, in the garb of a Walkyr, spear upraised and poised against an emasculated husband, clad as a Teutonic knight, spear limply at his side.

[32] James Thurber, *Men, Women, and Dogs*. (New York: Harcourt, Brace & Co., 1943.)

destructive of the mystery and wonder of it, as to have transformed the bond between sexuality and humanity into a battleground of relentless and interminable warfare. Mr. Thurber seems to be saying that dogs are at an enviable advantage over men and women because they have been spared this devastating and de-identifying conflict. He would give his life to be a dog, but is condemned to live with and live out his frustrating humanity. Steig and Steinberg have become at once more subtle and more articulate about this battle. Patriarchal and matriarchal tyrannies respectively deflower and castrate the humanity of sexual partners, who can neither escape each other nor bear to each other the identity of selfhood through a sexual relationship, at once basic, dependable and humanizing. Whether bitterly, or tongue-in-cheek, these sensitive observers of the sexual revolution of our time seem to be pressing an insistent question raised by the incongruity of human sexuality. That question is whether the conflict between the mystery and the threat of belonging is the sign of a dehumanizing fate foredooming sexuality to frustration and fear or of a frontier across which the possibility of joining freedom with responsibility in sexual experience and practice is at hand. At hand would be the possibility of the transfiguration of sexuality through the grace and truth of an humanizing faith.

The Transfiguration of Sexuality

It will occasion no surprise that a Christian look at the sexual revolution should sooner or later take a look at Jesus Christ. In doing so, at this point in our discussion, we do not affirm that the dynamics of the sexual revolution find their culmination in Jesus Christ. Too often, Christian faith and thought are offered as a simplistic answer to historical and human problems. The implication is that if everybody were Christian, the problems would disappear. The facts are that nobody can be compelled to become Christian, that everybody will not take up Christianity as "their thing," that other humanizing answers to the search for sexual meaning must be recognized, and that Christians are themselves not free of the perplexities and complexities of sexual experience and behavior. Our present concern is to follow the long biblical journey from the "image of God" to the "image of Christ," from creation to redemption, and to try to suggest how the search for sexual meaning may find in that journey a perspective and power through which freedom may be joined with responsibility in sexual experience and behavior. This perspective and power frankly involve the risk of believing as the companion of the risk of belonging. The risk of believing is the risk of openness to the presence of Christ in the heights and depths, the perplexities and complexities of human experience, and the risk of taking the risk of belonging in the context and the power of that commitment.[33] What, then, does the presence of Jesus Christ, in the experience of the Christian, offer to the experience and practice of human sexuality? The answer is: *the transfiguration of that experience through the transfiguration of the participants in it, as they participate in it.* Thus, sexual experience and behavior, as basic to humanity, become integral to discipleship. The ultimate escape, according to which experience is transfigured because people are transfigured, is blocked. Transfiguration joins experience and participants in a reciprocity which makes the sexual act the basic occasion of human renewal. *Transfiguration is the overshadowing of the threat of belonging by the gift of the mystery and wonder of belonging, owing to the presence of Jesus Christ in the search for sexual meaning.*[34] The presence of Jesus Christ is involved with sexual

[33] Thus, Bonhoeffer's maxim, which he applied to the situation of discipleship, we may apply to sexual experience and behavior. "This situation," Bonhoeffer wrote, "may be described by two propositions, both of which are equally true. Only he who believes is obedient, and only he who is obedient believes." See, Dietrich Bonhoeffer, *The Cost of Discipleship*, New York, The Macmillan Co., 1949, p. 56.

[34] This formulation is ventured in the light of the accounts of the transfiguration of Jesus. (Matthew 17:1-8; Mark 9:2-8; Luke 9:28-36) The Greek verb, μεταμορφόω (metamorphoō) is used here of Jesus, not in the sense of a deification of him, but in the sense of Jesus' presence as the bearer of an ultimate transformation already under way. Instructive also is the association of μετεμορφώθη (was transfigured) with being "covered with shadow" (ἐπεσκίασεν). The identical word is used to describe the action of the Holy Spirit in effecting the conception of the Virgin. Thus, the so-called "Virgin

experience and behavior—from *coitus* to fulfilling companionship —not as a conscious awareness but as the experience of joy and peace in belonging which seals and celebrates the giving and receiving of identity in faithfulness and freedom.

In an early, and not sufficiently heeded essay of Bonhoeffer's, a penetrating and succinct description of this experience occurs. It may be cited here, somewhat extensively, because it connects Adam and Christ, the image of God in its creation and in its restoration, and the sense in which the transfiguration of humanity has occurred. "To be in Adam," Bonhoeffer writes, is to be

"in untruth, in culpable perversion of the will . . . inwards to the self . . . Man has broken loose from communion with God, thus also with men, and now he stands alone, which is in untruth. Because he is alone, the world is 'his' world, his fellow-men have sunk into the world of things . . . for he is utterly 'by himself' in the falsehood of self-lordship. . . . The *everydayness* of man in Adam is guilt. It is the option for self isolation . . . It is the creature's wilful and compulsive quest for enjoyment, and as such it is constantly in flight from matters whose acknowledgement sets bounds to the business of enjoyment: death and oneself, as rightly known. But because flight is hopeless . . . the everydayness of Adam is desperation—and that all the more, the wilder the flight and the less man is conscious of despair. Superficiality is the mask of lonely isolation; it is directed lifeward, but its beginning and end is death and guilt."

To be in Christ, on the other hand, is "man . . . torn away from the attempt to remain alone with himself and . . . turned towards Christ. This is the gift of faith, that man no longer looks on himself but on salvation . . . which has come to him from without. . . . If, through man's self-incapsulation, *existence* (Dasein) in Adam was in subjection to the *quality* (Wiesein) of existence, the sight of Christ brings the loosening of the bonds: *existence* becomes free, not as if it were able to stand over against the *quality* of existence as independent being, but in the sense of escaping from the I's domination into the lordship of Christ, where for the first time in original freedom it recognizes itself as the creature of God. . . .

Birth" symbolizes among other things the transfiguration of sexuality with the coming of Jesus into the world of men and for humanity.

(To be in Christ is to be a) person whose existence has been affected, redirected or re-created by Christ." [35]

This shift from self-incapsulation to the freedom of creaturehood, applied to sexuality, means that the identity-freedom-fidelity
syndrome has begun to give shape to a structure of belonging within
which the sexual relation between male and female begins to function once again as the basis and bearer of what it takes to be human in the world. The risk of belonging, being deprived of its
threat, becomes the beginning of meaningful participation in all
life's creative occasions: "to fill the earth and conquer it." In the
context of this shift, sexual experimentation finds its appointed
place and limit in the finding, by male and female, each of the
other. Sexual experimentation belongs to the dynamics of identity
in freedom. It does not mean, in and of itself, that promiscuity has
made a sexual goal of passion. Nor does the limit appointed for
sexual experimentation mean the surrender of the mystery and
wonder of belonging to arbitrary social, moral and religious attempt to safeguard the sexual relation against the threat of belonging. The limit set for sexual experimentation is the limit set by the
structure of belonging upon the search for sexual meaning. This
search is perennially imperiled by a double desperation. On the
one hand, there is uncertainty about belonging; on the other hand,
there is disillusionment with belonging. The first leads to confusion and doubt about the possibility of finding the other; the second, leads to bitterness and self-deception about the possibility of
fulfillment with and through the other. Broadly speaking, the first
is a form of sexual despair before the commitments involved in
marriage have become part of sexual experience and behavior. The
second is a form of sexual despair which finds in marriage the futility and not the fullness of sexual experience and behavior. The
fundamental mistake of the moralization of sexual behavior is that

[35] Dietrich Bonhoeffer, *Act and Being*, New York: Harper & Row, 1956,
abridged from pp. 155, 156, 166, 170-171, 174. Italics are Bonhoeffer's; parentheses mine. Recall here, a possible congruence between "The everydayness of
man" and Sister Corita's to keep life "from being so daily."

it hopes to prevent the futility and failure of marriage by preventing the experimentation prerequisite to sexual commitments that make for belonging. Thus, the antidote to sexual despair is sought in the displacement of gospel by law, of freedom by conformity. And all the while, the human meaning of sexuality is being exiled from sexual experience and behavior.

But suppose the shift from being "in Adam" to being "in Christ" were made. How, then, would one deal with the question: How do I know when I have found the other to whom I belong? and with the question: How does one avoid disillusionment and find fulfillment in marriage? To the first question, the answer is that when the attraction to and by another is transfigured through the structure of belonging into the finding of the Other, then, the risk of belonging may be made because the threat of belonging has been enveloped and nourished by its mystery and wonder. To the second question, the answer is that when marriage is entered upon with the singleness of commitment rooted in the singleness of an ultimate faith, its disillusionments lose *their* ultimacy and its expectations become the source of ever fresh discoveries that the threat of belonging has been transfigured by its mystery and wonder. Monogamy without monotheism is precarious; and marriage without monogamy falls short of fulfillment.

These answers do not mean that sexual experimentation will unfailingly lead through the structure of belonging to the other; or that the shift from being "in Adam" to being "in Christ" excludes the dissolution of marriage through separation or divorce. There are no securities in sexual experience and behavior against the pain of failure or the suffering occasioned by the shattered possibility of sexual meaning and fulfillment. The transfiguration of sexuality by the presence and power of Christ means that the sexual revolution of our time is a way forward to the experience that sexuality and humanity belong together. Joy and peace in belonging are the fruit of joy and peace in believing.[36] For,

36 Romans 15:13.

"one's not half of two. Its two are halves of one:
which halves reintegrating, shall occur
no death and any quantity; . . .

. . .

one is the song which fiends and angels sing:
all murdering lies by mortals told make two.
Let liars wilt, repaying life they're loaned;
we (by a gift called dying born) must grow

deep in dark least ourselves remembering
love only rides his year.

All lose, whole find" [37]

[37] Copyright, 1944, by E.E. Cummings. Reprinted from his volume POEMS 1923-1954 by permission of Harcourt, Brace & World, Inc.

5

Questions of Life from
Questions of Death

•

G. R. DUNSTAN

We are disturbed, Canon Dunstan notes, in the transplant debates, about the fertility drugs, and in the talk about test-tube babies
and semen banks because these remind us of the animal in each of us.
But we have to accept our kinship with the animal order, and understand our relationship to it, before ethical thinking on these human
questions can begin. Canon Dunstan is professor of moral and social
theology at King's College, London, and also Priest in Ordinary to
Her Majesty The Queen. He is the author of *The Family Is Not
Broken* and *Not Yet The Epitaph,* and has edited *The Register of
Edmund Lacy, Bishop of Exeter 1420-1455.* He is editor of the
monthly journal, *Theology.*

THE PARTICULAR PROBLEMS thrown up by the most recent developments in medical skills, and by present medical research, are sometimes discussed too early in ethical and moral terms. A prior discussion is required, to determine something about the nature of man himself, before particular ethical questions can be discussed purposefully at all. In traditional language, thought has to begin with "Man: his Origin and Destiny." In an oblique way, there is much to be said for beginning the other way round—for coming to the vexed questions of life through the Christian understanding of death. Certainly, the discussion of some of our problems invariably comes to a stop when we realize the inadequacy of our theology of death.

Disce mori is a familiar motto on armorials: "Learn to die." *De Bono Mortis*, "On the good of death," is another—and the title of treatises, too. Why, for Christians, is death a "good"? It is a good because Christians believe that God has provided riches, a glory, for man of which he can have only glimpses, or foretastes, or—as Wordsworth put it—"intimations" in this mortal life. Death is not merely *inevitable* for him, not merely a snuffing out of life, from which he cannot escape. Death is *necessary* for him as a condition of entering upon this inheritance, this enjoyment of God's glory. This is why Jesus, in the Gospels, when speaking of his own death, did not speak of it as an inevitable risk, but as a *necessity*. He *had* to die: the death would consummate the life; and so he cried, "It is accomplished, fulfilled," at the moment of death. To die well, to make a good death, has, therefore, been entrenched in the tradition of Christian piety. "Burn now your candle as long as ye will: it has naught to do with me, for my light cometh when day breaketh." [1]

[1] Bede, *Eccl. Hist.* iv. 8; in Helen Waddell, *The Wandering Scholars;* Collins: Fontana Books, 1968, p. 64.

This coming glory, this perfection of character and relationship which we speak of as the life of the world to come, casts its light back on the living of life, and on its beginning. We were created for an end. We say that God made man in his own image. This does not mean that there is a physical likeness between God and man. It means that God made man to be capable of this glory: capable of responding to him, knowing him, and becoming like him; capable, as I have said, of perfection in character and relationship. This, in the language of Christian theology, is what gives man his unique status. It is this which opens to man his boundless opportunities: this also which sets him about with bounds—creates his ethics, speaks to him in terms of what he may do, must do, and must not do. The ethical questions of today would not arise without this presupposition that man is of great worth, of unique worth; and Christians ground the worth of man on these dogmas about his origin and his calling.

THE ANIMAL IN US

This presupposition, and these dogmas, have been embedded in the thought of the Christian world for a very long time. They have created certain attitudes and institutions: certain norms or expectations in custom, in the common law, and in the professional practice of doctors, nurses, social workers, and scientists engaged in research upon human beings and human affairs. The essential "humanity" of man, his distinctiveness and uniqueness, have therefore become axioms among us. It is precisely this axiom which has been shaken by events in the last few months and years. What has disturbed us, in the transplant debates, in the fertility drugs, and in the talk of semen banks and test-tube babies, is our being made to face the animal in us: to realize that, human and unique as we are, this humanity is lodged in, and expresses itself through, a body, a psycho-physical organism, rooted, by a network of the finest roots, in the sub-human world, the animal world, the world of organic life, of chemistry and molecules common to other forms of life and of matter.

Please observe: I am not repudiating the animal in us: I am suggesting that while normally—in all our characteristically human relations, and in the flights of the spirit in music, poetry, and the language of religion and of love—we glory in our humanity and forget the animal in us, now we are brought face to face with the animal, and we are taking a little time to grow used to what we see. It shakes us to think that the transplanting of human kidneys, or livers, or hearts is probably only a temporary expedient: because organs from an animal, transplanted into a human body, would do just as well, if and when the problem of immune rejection can be overcome. It shakes us when a human mother gives birth to what we might, without offence, call a litter. People worry about the use of machines to prolong artificially the pumping motion of the heart, in order to keep blood circulating through the brain and other organs: people worry about the person lying for long in a coma, whose heart and vital functions continue spontaneously, but whose brain has almost totally disintegrated or been destroyed— from whom, as we say, the personality has gone: people worry about the new uncertainties in determining, in some very few instances, the fact of death, even in understanding what death is. How different from that lovely peaceful first stanza in John Donne's poem, "A Valediction":

> "As virtuous men passe mildly away
> And whisper to their soules, to goe,
> Whilst some of their sad friends doe say,
> The breath goes now, and some say, no."

Different: but the same uncertainty was there. We worry about these things simply because they shake the confidence on which we rely for all our normal dealings, in our knowing what it is to be a human being, to be alive: they bring us face to face with the fact that we share the basic mechanism of our life with the animal and sub-animal world.

Now it is the duty of reasonable men—and their privilege—to look calmly at their worries, and not to be carried away by them. It is the duty of reasonable men—and among them I include Christian men—not to be swayed by hysteria or mass emotion, when events like these disturb them; not to panic because of temporary difficulties or occasional mistakes or miscalculations in an experimental period, and so encumber themselves with the wrong long-term remedies. Neither, on the other hand, do reasonable men conclude that because something can be done—because it is technically possible—it therefore ought to be done, or is desirably done. We know now how to blow up the world, with thermo-nuclear weapons; we aim to live with this technical possibility, without using it. We know equally of the possibilities of wideranging interference with the organic structure of man—from genetic manipulation and the intricacies of brain surgery to conditioning in all its forms; yet we have to determine, how much ought to be done, for whom, by whom, in what circumstances, subject to what conditions—and so on. The wider the possibilities, the greater the burden of ethical decision. Our uniqueness as men consists in our having the capacity, and the sense of obligation, to make these decisions. No other animal, so far as we know, carries this burden.

Controversies

At this point it would be possible to break out of the chain of reflection pursued so far—the paradox of man as both heaven-bound spirit and as animal, one of the creeping things of the earth—and offer some tabloid reflections upon the controversies of the day: the pill which prevents people from having babies and the pill which seems to give them a surprising number; the possibility of synthesizing life, that is, of growing a child as it were in a test-tube; the theoretical possibilities of genetic control offered by semen banks, artificial fecundation, the transfer of embryos from mother to mother (already practised in animal husbandry), even by cellular surgery and selection of genes; or, at the other end of the span, the artificial prolongation of life, the recognition or even accomplishment of death, the transplanting of organs, and the problem of distributing equitably a medical resource—like kidney dialysis—which is in short supply. All these subjects, and more, could invite consideration; and the most they could be given would be a paragraph or two on each. It seems more profitable, however, to follow out the logic of the paradox, and so to furnish the internal equipment (so to speak) with which these particular problems may be better analysed. Is man no more, in fact, than a naked ape? Is there no essential difference, in fact, between the baby in the incubator, watched over and fought for with all the resources of medical science, and the puppy contentedly sleeping in its mother's basket?

First, rather than deny the kinship between animal and man, I would suggest that we have still a long way to go in exploring their likeness, the resources which they have in common. It is revealing to attend a discussion by theologians of what they call "the doctrine of man" in the presence of, say, a Professor of Animal Behaviour. Again and again the theologians will assert some claim for man which sets him apart from the animals: and the Professor of Animal Behaviour would, on appeal, counter with some observation on the behaviour of animals or of birds which meant that the statement of the theologians, in as far as it was an empirical statement (i.e. a statement about something open to observation) could not be upheld. The patient study of animals and their behaviour—in themselves and for themselves—has only just begun. As it unfolds it will surprise us. It will, I predict, not tend to bring man down, to lead us to conclude that man is only an animal; it will tend to bring the animal up: to give us pause and make us examine very carefully the way in which we use our power over the animals, to make them serve our purpose, or even—and with shame we have to say it—our selfish pleasures.

Now already we use animals extensively in medical research. Animals are bred in captivity in order that we may test on them new drugs, new surgical experiments, new physical and psychological tests—none of which would we dare, now, to test on human beings until we were fairly convinced that they were relatively safe and held some promise of qualified success. In Great Britain the regulations and controls governing experiments on living animals are strict, and the general ethical standard of medical research workers toward their animals is high. It is not so everywhere, and there is disquiet in the profession at the way animal life is squandered in so-called research, particularly in countries which can afford prodigality in their research: but that is not my point at present. This research is conducted on the supposition of a close likeness between the animal organism and the human organism: without that supposition, no valid lessons for humans could be drawn from research upon animals. It follows that the nearer the animal comes to our scale of human responses, especially neurological responses, so—it would seem to me—the nearer the animal comes also to a claim to that protection and consideration which we allow to the human being. Our extending knowledge of animal behaviour must extend also our ethical concern for the creatures on whom we experiment: otherwise we shall, before long, grow even more confused about the ethics of our experiments with man. We need, in short, some understanding of man's place in nature before we are able fully to understand man; we need some understanding of the extent and limitations of man's lordship or dominion over nature before we can determine what man may properly do to those of his own kind.

This is the unresolved question which has caused the controversy about the papal encyclical, *Humanae Vitae.* The controversial core of that encyclical is its restatement of the now traditional Roman Catholic doctrine that "each and every marriage act must remain open to the transmission of life" (paragraph 11); thus excluding, in the words of paragraph 14, "every action which, either in anticipation of the conjugal act, or in its accomplishment, or in the development of its natural consequences, proposes, whether as an end or as a means, to render procreation impossible." Dom David Knowles, writing in defence of the encyclical in *The Tablet* of 5 October, 1968, interprets these judgments in a significant way:

> "The physical process and the human love . . . are, in God's design, indissolubly linked, and to put one of these (either the love or the physical process) out of action, or to prevent the possibility of the physical action having the consequence for which it exists

throughout the animal creation, is to thwart the design of the Creator."

These are carefully measured words, and they deserve respect, coming as they do from so great a scholar and teacher. But you will observe where they lead us: they bind human begetting inextricably with animal begetting:

> "to prevent the possibility of the physical action having the consequence for which it exists *throughout the animal creation* is to thwart the design of the Creator."

The act of human begetting, Dom David says (quite rightly) must not take place in separation from the human love: but when it does take place, it has precisely the status of reproduction in animals, no more, no less.

Now this represents a very sophisticated and subtle view of man indeed, and one which, in broad outline, is highly defensible in terms of Christian theology: it affirms totally man's creaturehood, and his biological kinship with the animal creation; it affirms also man's spiritual capacities, including the capacity to love in a fully human way, and, indeed, to transmute human love into a "sacramental" union. But the question which we have to press—and which Roman Catholic critics of the encyclical also press—is whether this statement does justice to all the truth about man, and to all the truth about man's relation to the animal creation.

Dom David has already allowed that man differs from the animal in his capacity to subordinate sexual union to a relationship of love. He would, following the encyclical, allow other differences: that in man the desire and capacity for sexual union arise independently of the times when fecundation is possible—as they do not in animals; and that man, having knowledge of this, has learned to recognize *two* functions in the act of union, not simply one: they are the deepening of the personal union of the spouses, and the begetting of offspring. But, again following the teaching of the encyclical, he would not allow man to act upon that knowledge, to separate the two processes: if the act is performed at all, it must be allowed all its animal consequences. The one concession which the encyclical itself makes to this knowledge—a concession which, many would argue, overthrows the whole logic of the central prohibition—is to allow married people deliberately to calculate when to expect the days of animal infertility, and to enjoy their sexual union, for its unitive purpose alone, during those days. This is to subordinate the characteristically human to the characteristically animal.

To critics of the encyclical, this is an intolerable restriction upon the range of human judgment, of human lordship or dominion over the animal creation—over the animal ingredient in ourselves. If we may use for a moment the language of the Creation myth in Genesis, the same voice which said "Be fruitful and multiply" said also "Let man have dominion over the fish of the sea, and over the birds of the air, and over the cattle, and over all the earth, and over every creeping thing that creeps upon the earth." By pronouncing man to be a creature made in the image of God, this same voice gave a profound, even eternal significance to every child of man, made each one a precious thing, of infinite worth. It is open for anyone to *say* that the bringing of these precious souls to birth is the one area of human activity in which man must suspend his dominion: in which he must leave everything to biological chance (for this is what language about "consequences throughout the animal kingdom" means) but the proposition is not self-evident: it has to be proved. And many there are who would deny it. By implication the Lambeth Conferences of 1958 and 1968 did deny it, summing up a *consensus* already found throughout the Anglican Communion. They affirmed that it is the responsibility (not merely a thing permitted) of Christian parents to exercise their conscientious judgment about the number and frequency of the conceptions of their children, and it left them at liberty to choose the means which, all things considered, they themselves believed to be most apt to that end. Other non-Roman churches had made similar affirmations. The whole debate upon contraception—excluding much on which both sides are agreed, about the purposes of marriage, and the dangers of abuse—turns precisely on this question of the degree of man's lordship in nature: upon the question how far may he act upon his knowledge to take control of organic processes—what I have loosely called "the animal"—in order to direct them to specifically human ends which he himself chooses and thinks good to pursue?

This is the main question as the test to be applied to those problems on the frontiers of death and life of which we are now so conscious. Those problems could not have arisen except for the progress of medical knowledge and skill; and medical knowledge and skill could not have advanced as they have but for the progress of experimental scientific research.

HUMANITY AND INHUMANITY

In asserting—as I have by implication—that man has a lordship over the organic world, even over the *humanized processes* of the organic world (like the characteristic acts of human sexual love), have I appeared to suggest that man's dominion is absolute? that there are no limits to what he may do, either with animals or with himself and his fellow men? I hope not. For the chief paradox about man emerges precisely when we think about this: the paradox that, in the searching judgment which he has the capacity to pass upon himself, he knows a category of acts which he calls "inhuman"—and he places into that category of inhuman acts many things which can be done, and have been done, in the name of science, in the very assumption of this unlimited power over animals and men. He has, in his long history, devised codes of conduct to regulate medical behaviour—from the Hippocratic code of ancient Greece to the Helsinki Declaration of the World Medical Association in 1964. These codes may well be explored in terms of this formula of man's likeness and unlikeness to the animal creation, to discern the presuppositions on which they rest.

Man is part of this creation, yet stands above it. Therefore his organic processes are as much a proper subject for scientific investigation as any other part of the natural order: and yet, because he is man, there must be special conditions and limitations attaching to it. (And because of the closeness, or kinship, of some of the animal creation to man, man in his more humane moments extends some of those special conditions and limitations to these animals also). In modern medicine then, based on scientific research as it is, man is both a *patient* and an *object* of scientific investigation. The doctor is both physician—concerned for the good of his patient—and a scientific investigator, concerned with observation, and the testing of hypotheses, and the pursuit of knowledge and the development of skill. Since all patients are, in some sense, unique, every medical treatment, however simple, is experimental. By trial and error the doctor learns—first, what will most help his patient, secondly, whatever can be learnt which may help other patients, or prevent them from becoming patients. This is the stuff of life, in daily medical practice: the means by which medical skills have grown, and are still growing; the means by which all those interventions in the processes of birth, life and death which create our present problems have become possible. More possibilities lie in the future. They rest on the normal presuppositions of the scientific method—that we can learn by investigation, and can formulate what we learn, and use our knowledge to improve man's lot: to carry him forward, in a way, to a new stage in his development, his evolution.

But are there characteristics in man which set limits to what may be done to him, in the name of science, even in the name of medicine? Our own consciences—the consciences of scientists and of doctors, not simply of theologians and philosophers—tell us that there are. Man is unique—with a uniqueness open to scientific observation and description, not simply a uniqueness resting upon theological assertion, a dogma uttered in the name of God. He is capable of reflection; of moral reflection; and so of judgment, moral judgment—of pronouncing actions right or wrong. He is capable of consenting to experiments upon himself, or of refusing this consent; and he makes this moral judgment that what he claims to exercise himself—the right of consent—he must allow to others. He insists that such consent must be free, and based on as much truthful information as can be conveyed. He knows that there is part of himself which is real, but which cannot be reduced

to the terms of scientific description—we call it the realm of the
spirit, for want of a better term; a part which cannot be satisfied
with any material satisfactions, but only with those which we call
spiritual. These satisfactions he realizes in relationships, and cannot have without them: the relationships themselves are therefore
sacred, in the sense that science must stop at the threshold, if by
entering it would violate them. So we allow rights to kindred, to
spouses, to parents and children; even to friends. Husband and
wife are in law one person: one cannot be compelled (in the common law) to give evidence in court against another. The controversies about who should consent to the removal of an organ for
transplanting, after death, centre upon this fact of relationships,
this sense of a real interest generated by relationship even in the
dead body of another person,

> "Think not the end, that from my body frees me,
> Breaks and unshackles me from thee.
> Triumphs the soul above its house in ruin,
> Deathless, begot of immortality." [2]

(I do not intend by these words to declare myself *against* those
surgeons who want to simplify the process of getting permission for
the transplant of organs: I am only pointing out what is the central fact at issue, adding only that the interest in the dead may
become excessive, even obsessional, and is by no means absolute.)
Among these relationships, essential for the full development of
the humanity of man, is the relationship with God. In the last
analysis, all that is done to or for a man must be judged by this
question—though I confess that I seldom stop to ask it—"How
far will this act, or treatment, help him and those about him in
the furtherance of their relationship with God?"

You may think this unfair, that it is too much to ask of the
doctor or the natural scientist. I am encouraged to find that Teilhard de Chardin did not think so. He, in a short piece, asked the
question: "Can biology taken to its extreme limit enable us to
emerge into the transcendent?" [3]

[2] Paulinus of Nola, *Carmina* xi; in Helen Waddell, *op. cit.*, p. 38.
[3] Teilhard de Chardin, *Science and Christ*; Collins, 1968, p. 212.

In other words, is man's final and eternal destiny integrally related to the evolutionary process, or must there come a stop to the process and then an irrelevant leap into the transcendent? He answered that the biological process can and must enable us to emerge into the transcendent. His words only restate my question in another form: how far will this act or treatment help the man and those about him in the furtherance of their relationship with God? And this in the Christian view is the final question. Evade it as we will throughout life we have to face it in the universal fact of death. Not all men would pose the question in these words, but all who think seriously about what they are doing with men must face it in some words or other, or else admit frustration. Struggle as they will, give as they will of the utmost of their humanity, of their costly skill, of their knowledge penetrating into the central mysteries of life, give all, do all—and some day the man to whom it is given, the man for whom it is done, will die. This must be a daunting, frustrating fact for them, did they not believe that, despite his close involvement in the world of matter and in the animal creation, this human being transcends them all; that as a human being he finds his meaning and his ultimate satisfaction only in relation to some absolute being outside himself—a relation which gives him unique value from the moment when his can be called a life, to the moment when it must be said, the life is gone.

6

Sex in Biblical Perspective

•

OTTO A. PIPER

We may not expect the moral aspect of sex to be stated by means of a uniform, universal and unchanging set of moral principles except in the purely formal Commandment, "Thou shalt not commit adultery"—this is the finding of Dr. Piper in his biblical essay. Dr. Otto A. Piper is professor of New Testament literature and exegesis at Princeton Theological Seminary. He is the author of many books including *The Biblical View of Sex and Marriage, The Christian Interpretation of Sex, Protestantism In The Ecumenical Age,* and *Die Grundlagen der Evangelischen Ethik.*

•

In contemporary Protestant ethics, it is sexual ethics in particular that receives the most attention. Within the churches and congregations no agreement has been reached on that subject, and, what is more, there is utter confusion concerning the basic issues and standards. The older generation is inclined to emphasize the institutional approach according to which sex and marriage are correlated. Premarital and extramarital intercourse are therefore condemned as being morally wrong.

Modern Approaches

The crudeness of that position is patent. Moral goodness is thereby identified with adherence to a legal institution. For that view, idealism offers a remedy. In idealistic humanism, of which Schleiermacher was the principal promoter, it is held that through love, sex is transformed from a purely physiological phenomenon into a moral attitude. Since such an outlook seems to combine the psychological reality with a lofty metaphysical perspective, many Protestant theologians are inclined to consider humanism the specifically Christian outlook. Unfortunately, however, such a view not only is unable to do justice to the marital institution, but also fails to establish an intrinsic relation between love and sex.

In modern "situational ethics," love is identified with sexual sympathy and thus lacks motivating power as a moral incentive. In turn, in its idealistic understanding, love is regarded as personal sympathy which is morally desirable, yet is not specifically related to sex. Its goal might therefore be reached apart from sexual relations. The Freudian idea, according to which sexual desire may be sublimated into love, will be true only when love is understood as sympathy with a person who proves to be a source of pleasure for

98

me. That may be practical wisdom in certain circumstances, yet falls short of imparting a moral aspect to sex.

Over against these endeavors to confer ethical dignity on sex by combining it with heterogeneous factors such as marriage or humanistic love, the younger generation, inside the churches as well as outside, will argue that sex is an integral portion of a person's natural life. Sex for them is to be enjoyed like other goods of nature and not subject to moral restraints, provided only that the sexual relation rests upon mutual consent. It is with a certain uneasiness, however, that the younger generation adopts this attitude. Sexual relation may entail pregnancy, and thus the cry for the "pill" as a general contraceptive. Furthermore, a youth who through film and television has been familiarized with homosexuality, seduction of children and sexual abnormalities, is not so certain that sex in all its manifestations should be regarded as natural and permissible. Likewise, while expressing belief in the sanctity of matrimony, the adult members of our churches are not so sure whether all extra-marital relationships are to be condemned. Not to all stories which glamorize passion in modern literature and the movies do they react with harsh indignation. It is obvious that by itself sexual desire does not provide moral guidance.

THE ONTOLOGICAL BASIS OF ETHICS

This universal uneasiness and uncertainty must be taken as an indication that Protestant ethics is confronted by more than a question of theological methodology. There is a new experience that must be taken seriously. In order to cope with that problem in a satisfactory way it is necessary to realize two facts.

First, modern theological ethics requires a scientific treatment. It cannot simply be built upon the social practice of the church. Such a pragmatic approach was legitimate as long as the church was a relatively homogeneous entity which had its authoritative center in the clergy and in Christian mores. In the present phase of history, however, the church is weakened by secularization and fragmentation. Hence the ethical standards are to be sought in superior determinants. Ethical motivation is not primarily to be found in biblical or confessional commandments, but rather in the structures of reality from which those commandments derived their validity.

Secondly, we have to realize that in the realm of sex the church is confronted with a new outlook. While in a certain sense it may be said that sex is sex and does not change throughout the ages, consciousness about sex, which characterizes modern life, differs radically from that of the Victorian man or certainly the medieval man. In the past, sex was experienced as an intriguing mystery, vexing and inescapable yet incomprehensible and thus to be kept on the very fringe of consciousness or rendered innocuous by means of ribald stories. Today the nude body and its anatomy are familiar to our children. For modern man sex is a biological fact which is publicly discussed in all its details. Thus it may be explained in a detached and scientific way.

At this point, however, the question arises whether or not the detached treatment of sex, which is given in biology or psychology, does justice to what is experienced by two people engaged in sexual relations. We contend that the scientific treatment of sex isolates it from actual experience. It deals with the proximate factors which constitute an object as it is given to our sense perception. Yet, in order to understand the very meaning of our experience we must observe its objects in the relation in which they stand to our personal life, on the one hand, and to their determinants on the other. Sex must be seen in the light of what is going on in the two people concerned. Sexual experience is not the product of myself, but rather that which takes hold of me, as it were, from outside myself.

The fundamental weakness of the contemporary naturalistic approach to sexual ethics lies in the assumption that it is morally right merely because it is in agreement with the biological or psychological view of sex. At the same time it is to be kept in mind that we are not simply concerned with sex as a general human phenomenon. Rather both adults and youth are obviously wrestling with the moral problem that originates in their being members of the church. The adults are not satisfied with a life lived in conformity with the moral tradition of the church. What stirs them up and frequently worries them is the question, In what way is the church's view of sex related to the rest of our faith? Is Christian sexual ethics a mere appendix to our spiritual life, or does it form an essential portion of it?

In these circumstances a mere restatement of the sexual ethics of the past would be futile. What is required is a model of human life which does not rely on metaphysical postulates. Man is not only to be seen in his natural context, but also in his relation to God. The biblical view of sex has so frequently been misinterpreted in recent times because exegetes substituted the naturalistic model of man for the biblical one.

THE BIBLICAL MODEL

1. *Man*

Following the classical Greek tradition of anthropology, the modern scientist is prone to consider man as a composite being, whose organs, faculties and abilities are but loosely connected and exist more or less independent of each other. The Bible, however, regards man an integral being in which everything conditions everything else, and all actions are manifestations of man's ego. As a result, sex is not treated as an incidental bodily function, but rather as a process that affects the self. This view is confirmed by the close relationship between irregularities and malfunctions of sexual life, on the one hand, and physiological and mental troubles, on the other. Even a person's character and his way of thinking may be tangibly influenced thereby. Thus, Jesus can point out that sexuality is not confined to coitus but rather is one's way of reacting to and dealing with the other sex. Likewise, it is more than an oriental exaggeration, when as cure against sexual temptations, Jesus recommends cutting off one's hand and pulling out one's eye (Mt. 5:27-30). Sexual desire is not caused by the organs of procreation but originates in the nature of the individual as a member of the animal realm and can be combated only by rejecting the claim which our existence here on earth makes on us.

Another characteristic feature of human nature, by which our sexuality is determined, is the differentiation of the sexes. Strange to say, most writers dealing with sex fail to pay attention to the fact that sex is a relationship that is normally established between a male and a female. The individual is not self-sufficient in his sexuality. The importance of the interdependence of the two sexes is expounded in Gen., Ch. 2. Masculinity and femininity are not meaningful in themselves. Biblical religion rejects therefore both the phallic religions in which life is thought of as derived from the male semen, as also the mother religions in which the maternal womb or the goddess' breasts are worshiped as the source of life. The fact that sexual differentiation is explained at the beginning of the Bible and in connection with the creation of man, indicates the fundamental significance which the interrelation between the sexes has for human history and development. Unlike primitive religions, the Bible ascribes no special significance to the anatomical correspondence of penis and vagina. Rather the differentiation of the sexes is wholesome for mankind. If man were an agent of non-sexual procreation man would consider himself the source of life and thus a being like God (Gen. 2:18). But man is not an end in himself. He is destined by God to execute his creator's plan. The work demanded of man has two aspects which are implied in sexual differentiation. Both activity and receptivity are required in compliance with the divine plan, as symbolized by the respective roles of man and woman in sexual intercourse. Neither function is superior to the other one. The woman is meant to be the man's helper and fellow worker. Nor is it by any merit of either of them that they have that specific function. While he is asleep, that is to say, incapable of acting himself spontaneously, God makes out of his substance a fellow worker who is like himself and yet different. (Gen. 2:21) Thus, theirs is a common work in which they supplement each other.

The insufficiency of human nature seen in its undifferentiated condition does not lie in the mere lack of a companion. If that were the trouble with man, God might have made many Adams. The sexual differentiation points rather to the fact that man lives in an environment which he is to change and which changes him.

In the act of cohabitation, Adam recognizes not only the interdependence of the sexes (Gen. 4:1), but also the value which his mate has for him. The Bible makes relatively little of erotic love, which rests on the physical qualities and charms of the partner. By way of contrast, marital love is underscored. Through marriage, the spouses are capable of performing a common work in the service of God. That it is what makes them lastingly and profoundly dear to each other.

2. Sex and Creation

In the modern approach to sex people seem to be satisfied with the fact that man has sex. It is assumed that sex is a moral value for no more reason than that it exists. Many theologians, too, treat sex as an ultimate; they confine the task of sexual ethics to an investigation of the limits within which sex will operate in harmony with the development of one's personality, or with social life. To the biblical writers, however, sex is no end in itself. Ours is a world in which all things exist for each other and the whole universe. Sex is closely related to and deeply rooted in the fact that the world in which we live serves a divine purpose. Unless there were a creative power by which things were brought into existence, and by which they were ultimately determined, the existence of this world would make no sense. If this world had somehow brought itself into existence, it would also be free to alter itself if it desired so to do. The work of the Creator is manifested in the fact that this is a world which is constantly in motion and constantly in decomposition. Yet it not only constantly preserves its equilibrium, but also maintains its structure as basically unalterable. In it the generic and specific features do set narrow limits to individual mutations. While we are free to use or misuse our abilities, the consequences differ radically.

One implication of that cosmic order is the fact that in coitus the male semen is brought into contact with the female ovum, and that thereby the possibility of a new human being is established. The "modern" ethics denies the essential connection of sex and procreation and takes the latter as an evil concomitant that is to be precluded. There are reasons, of course, for occasionally preventing conception in certain phases of married life. The Roman Catholic doctrine, too, which absolutely forbids the use of contraceptives, is based upon "natural law." For Catholics procreation is dealt with as an end in itself. Such a view misses the biblical understanding of sex as much as does the "modern" view.

The creative will of God is not confined to the immutability of cosmic structures and essences, however. It also exhibits a teleological tendency, that is, all things in this world serve a divine purpose. That fact is seen in the world's self-preservation, its unending motion and the constant restoration of the cosmic equilibrium. Most conspicuously the telic character appears in the nisus of the organic world which, despite mortality, permanently reproduces itself. Man in particular is a creature who incessantly seeks satisfaction in his spontaneous actions.

It is in such a world and as such a creature that man is bound to envisage sex. The pleasure which it provides cannot be considered its final goal. The urge of the sexual desire must be considered also as an incentive to participate in the procreation of a new generation. The telic nature of sex is not to be sought in subjective desire. Rather, that desire is the subjective manner in which the species homo sapiens keeps itself in existence. In thus providing for the permanent existence of human beings, sex has its legitimate and necessary place in this world.

In turn, the instrumental character of sex explains the ambivalence of the institution of marriage. Apart from it no satisfactory provision can be found for the upkeep of the younger generation. Yet, in order to reach that goal marriage must be more than an occasion for legitimate sexual intercourse. Its moral value lies in its being for married couples the prerequisite of healthy social life. Through insisting upon the reciprocal relationship of husband and wife and through extending that relationship to the common responsibility for the upbringing of the children, biblical religion has created a specific type of family life. The attitudes and practices learned therein have proved to foment such civic virtues as regard for the equality of others, constructive political attitudes, bearing with each other's weakness or respect for the established order. While sexuality does not create them, they would not come into being apart from the sexual foundation of the family.

Such development is rendered possible by the fact that biblical religion recognizes and accepts the privileged role which man performs in the cosmos. The telic nature of the other organisms is confined to their ability to reproduce themselves (Gen. 1:22). Man is the only creature to whom a task has been assigned in this world (Gen. 2:15). In humanism, however, that task is mistakenly interpreted as self-realization, that is to say the cultivation and refinement of his abilities. Humanism considers the fact that man lives in the universe as a purely incidental feature, whereas what really matters is his selfhood as a spontaneous being. As Gen. Ch. 1 shows, nevertheless, biblical religion starts from the fact that the universe is as real as man, and man's task consists in transforming this world in order to make it a suitable habitat for mankind. In modern literature sex is overemphasized as though it were the only means by which life may be rendered meaningful, while in fact it is only a prerequisite of true life. Biblical religion overcomes the primitive notion that the sexual act is an indispensable means of self-fulfillment, yet also the medieval idea that sexual abstinence is morally superior to marriage. Christianity has comprehended the mystery of celibacy. By jumping the sexual stage of human existence, the individual realizes that the ultimate goal of man is not to be found in his physical existence but rather in his ability to be moved by God's spirit. Celibacy then is not a moral duty but rather a sign of the pursuit of the goal assigned to man.

Christianity has held celibacy in high esteem because it showed convincingly that life's satisfaction is not to be sought in the techniques of *ars amandi* (the art of loving).

Man is made in the image of God (Gen. 1:27). He is the creature through whom the plan which God has with this world is to be executed. Practically that means first of all, as the early church learned from the example of Jesus, that the idea of male hegemony in social life has a pagan background. Granting political equality to women should not be understood as meaning that in public life women should imitate the ways in which men act. The specific function for which women are destined in public life should rather be that of correcting and supplementing the inevitable self-centeredness of an exclusively male rule. In particular, the women in their receptiveness, will add openness for other people's idiosyncrasies and their needs, where the men tend one-sidedly to be interested in the pursuit of their plans. Moreover, in the light of mankind's divinely assigned task it will be seen that the reciprocal relation of the sexes is not confined to a floating moment of sexual intercourse. It will disclose its usefulness only when a lasting union is established. That is the reason why sex cannot be treated adequately except within the framework of marriage and family. Sexual promiscuity is based upon the assumption that the partner is to serve primarily as an instrument through whom sexual pleasure may be obtained, while the very significance which the other person might have for a partner in common pursuits is disregarded. The tone of bitterness and disappointment which characterizes the description of sexual love in modern literature eloquently proves the futility of self-assertion sought in unbridled sexuality.

In turn, when sex is incorporated into a life by which God's goal is pursued, sex is no longer a merely physiological urge of which an educated person should be ashamed. Rather, it has been sanctified by God. As Paul in Eph. 5:32 states, the institution of marriage foreshadows and symbolizes the ultimate mystery of life, namely, God's relation to mankind. That does not mean, as is contended by naturalistic ethics, that sex is morally good by itself and indulgence in it is always justified, or that as a legal institution marriage is a holy relationship. In the verse quoted above, Paul reminds his readers that the meaning of marriage is to be learned from Christ's relationship to the church. Only when seen in the light of our divine destination is the sexual relation sanctified. By saying that sex derives its meaning and standards of use from the fact that God has set to man a definite and inescapable goal, we give first of all expression to a general experience. Sex life makes no real sense unless it is related to a trans-subjective end. All attempts to mold sexual life exclusively by the individual's wishes and desires prove to be unsatisfactory. Positively, by referring to the revealed character of biblical commandment we mean that the standards by which sex is to be practiced are rooted in the nature of human life. They are not merely the result of rational deliberations. Hence, we may not expect the moral aspect of sex to be stated by means of a uniform, universal and unchanging set of moral principles except in the purely formal way of the commandment, "Thou shalt not commit adultery." Reality precedes knowledge. In accordance with deepened insights the significance of sexual life and the means by which its goal is to be reached, sexual ethics will differ from country to country and from generation to generation, even within the church. Yet the result is not a moral relativism. Related to historical experience the interpretation of the Law remains valid as long as that experience is not supplanted by a new and deeper one. A fresh generation may, for instance, denounce moral legalism in sexual conduct and the purely institutional view of marriage. Our youngsters may plead instead for personal responsibility and avoidance of sham appearance in marital relations though it may thus seem to destroy the whole fabric of social order. Such attitude may be legitimate, provided it is sufficiently realistic to take all aspects of sexual life seriously and is willing to learn from the experience of other members of the church, too.

3. *The Insufficiency of Earthly Life*

As a rule, the biblical writers refer to sexual life and its manifestations in a descriptive rather than an imperative manner. Quite particularly in the Sermon on the Mount, Jesus illustrates the meaning of the divine commandments. Understood literally the interpretation of the Old Testament Law which is offered by Jesus in Mt., Ch. 5, is absurd and unacceptable. Jesus seems to invalidate the Law by indicating that its implications make no sense in practical life. Yet by doing so, Jesus wants to point out that the moral imperatives are to be interpreted as indicating man's divine destination, and its eventual implementation. Presented as given by God, the moral commandments describe the kind of life for which man was made. Even if no man were ever able to keep them, they have therefore to be recognized as telling us what man should be like.

Here lies the fundamental difference between biblical ethics, on the one hand, and philosophical or natural ethics, on the other. The latter starts from the assumption that man is morally good by nature, though in his actual life he may be mistaken concerning his obligations. Presented as divine demands, the biblical commandments imply that without divine assistance they cannot be kept.

This does not mean that for man, moral goodness is unattainable. It implies, however, that man's supreme obligation is to be aware of his goal. How closely he will approximate it depends on a number of factors which are beyond his control. Naturalism rightly emphasizes that the pleasurable sensation conveyed by sex is not morally evil as was held by the ancient church fathers. But man misses the true understanding of his life when he considers that pleasure is the basis of true life.

This interpretation of the place which sex holds in moral life needs to be supplemented in two respects: Christians may miss their destination either out of ignorance, or for lack of moral strength. What is so often criticized or bewailed as sexual consciousness is in many cases the result of moral confusion. Young people may not have been made aware of the final goal of life and of the relation in which sex stands to our destination. When sex is treated as a biological phenomenon, it is not surprising that it is considered relevant merely as a source of pleasure. The prevailing anti-teleological philosophies, especially Positivism and Existentialism, are largely responsible for the moral confusion of our age. It is obvious that people who are preconditioned in that way, will be unable to derive from sexual intercourse the knowledge therein implied.

That does not mean that extramarital intercourse is altogether valueless. It may convey deep and extremely elating experiences. But it is not by chance that as long as sex is treated as an end in itself such lofty experiences alternate with sadness, disappointment, despair and even disgust. Such consequences are not surprising; for a self-contained erotic love implies contempt of the gift that God wants to impart to us through that one person with whom we are sexually united.

In addition to what people fail through ignorance in their sexual relations, the Bible mentions weak faith as the cause of dissatisfaction. Though man does not automatically move toward the goal which God has assigned to him, the imperative grammatical form of the commandment implies that the goal may be reached. What would be impossible on the basis of our natural equipment, may be performed by the power of the Spirit. When that assistance is spurned and rejected or when its power is doubted, the only device by which to safeguard one's moral self-respect is by lowering the goal in order to justify one's failures. That is what happens in a good deal of sexual ethics in modern Protestantism. Yet experience will also show that with such apologetic methods the serious character of sex is not removed. As a rule the problem is merely shifted from the provisional area of premarital life to that of marriage.

Yet, neither the ethicist nor the guardian of church mores has a right to look at sex as though it were other people's problem only. By familiarizing his disciples with the subtle manifestations of egotism, Jesus wanted to instruct them about the necessity of noticing truthfully their shortcomings when assailed by their egotism. Hence regard for the sexual mores of the congregation and decency will not suffice to render a Christian life meaningful. While we must rightfully deplore the dissolution of the social fabric, we ought not to conceal from ourselves the fact that the cause of the present chaos lies in our own egotism no less than in the young people's craving for freedom and the happiness of a full life.

According to historical circumstances, man's egotism will manifest itself in various areas of life, sometimes for instance as will for power or craving for wealth, and at other times as contempt for one's neighbors or desire of unrestricted freedom. In our age it seem to be the lust for sex and money that drives people crazy. Therapy for such ills must go to their root, namely, man's belief in his autonomy and self-sufficiency. A psychological or medical approach to the ailing area will bring momentary relief only.

Repentance is required above everything else. We must realize that it is by our own fault that sex has become such a problem for our age. We regard happiness our supreme good and pretend to be capable by our own strength and resources to find real satisfaction in life. Of course, we are reluctant to assume such an attitude because it seems to threaten us with the loss of deeply moving delight. There is no good reason for such apprehension. The only change will be in the appraisal of the partner. Rather than being the source of passing pleasure he will become a lifelong companion. Through that vision, family life will be radically transformed. It will be the fulfillment of God's plan according to which human life is one of mutual concern. Strengthened by that vision, family life will be life in truth. Temptations may not be lacking. Christians may also be carried away at times by unfriendliness, injustice and even unfaithfulness. But the determination to serve God's goal enables the followers of Jesus to call wrongness wrongness instead of disguising it as naturalness.

Repentance, however, is not effective without forgiveness. If individual life has no meaning by itself but rather finds it in reciprocal fellowship, repentance must be coupled with forgiveness, both by asking for it and by granting it to those who have hurt or harmed us. Forgiveness is not a purely mental transaction between two persons. God has made it the prerequisite of the remission of our sins. Implied in the cosmic order is the fact that all wrongdoing, once performed, will continue to harm both the perpetrator and his environment. God's pardon, however, radically changes the situation. When we repent and forgive others, God can render ineffective the harmful consequences of our faults. When the teleological relation of sex and family is recognized, the family becomes the place where forgiveness can be practiced in the most natural way. Thereby the family is in a position to become the nucleus of a new society. Of course, the Bible reminds its readers of the fact that both as individuals and as collectivity God's people have frequently lost sight of their ultimate goal. But by imploring the help and illumination of God's Spirit, their efforts in transforming human lives were not entirely in vain. Rather than bewailing our moral weakness and our lack of perfection we should encourage and strengthen each other in our endeavors to keep the vision of the new life burning in the church. Such an attitude will radically differ from mere acquiescence in the ambiguity of the sexual mores of the church. It implies a tangible and effective protest against all sexual practice which is meant to satisfy individual and tribal egotism. Yet it does so less by way of reprehension and censure than by setting an example of faith. It is the grandeur of the Christian life that notwithstanding its imperfections, and even through them, reverence for the divine goal is brought to light.

7

The Catholic Tradition for Responsibility in Sexual Ethics

•

JOHN L. THOMAS

Noting that it is becoming increasingly difficult for the major religious faiths in America to demonstrate relevance of their beliefs to sexual ethics, Fr. John L. Thomas, S.J. frankly discusses his own Catholic tradition, its problems at this point and its need for a reassessment. Fr. Thomas, who is research associate at the Cambridge Center for Social Research, then hazards a prediction or two. He is the author of numerous titles in this field: *The American Catholic Family, Marriage and Rhythm, The Family Clinic, The Catholic Viewpoint on Marriage and the Family,* and *Looking Toward Marriage.*

THE PROFOUND MALAISE pervading the current climate of opinion regarding sex reflects a vague general awareness of an unresolved moral crisis. It would be superficial to view the present state of uncertainty and confusion as little more than perplexed concern with the personal maladjustments or transitory social imbalances resulting from lags or delays in adapting traditional ways of thinking and acting to the shifting requirements of our technologically advanced urban environment. Rather it is becoming increasingly clear that we have finally succeeded in rejecting past "Victorian" or "Jansenist" sexual attitudes and norms only to discover we lack a commonly acknowledged framework of beliefs and values on the basis of which we can construct acceptable new goals and standards. Where there is no agreement on basic values, there is likely to be little agreement on practical programs of action. Conflicting moral ideologies tend to neutralize each other in the public forum, while the concerted effort needed for shared thinking and acting is paralyzed by the divergence of opinions.

Rapidly changing, complex, pluralist societies like our own, by placing the burden of choice wholly on the individual, make heavy demands on their participants. At a minimum, responsible decision-making requires some understanding of relevant facts, value premises, available alternatives and their consequences. The current malaise regarding sex should serve to remind us that failure to provide these prerequisites of responsible decision-making can prove just as frustrating and destructive of personal freedom as the arbitrary imposition of external restraints on its exercise.

Although it may offer us little consolation, it is well to recall that all known human societies have experienced difficulties in dealing with sex. None have been wholly successful in devising rational solutions, though past approaches have run the gamut from denigration and Stoic rejection to quasi-worship and Dionysian acceptance. Most have had to allow for a considerable degree of "patterned deviation" in the form of such openly tolerated discrepancies between theory and practice as the double standard, prostitution, mistresses, and relative promiscuity among various disenfranchised classes. We have very limited empirically based information on the sexual mores of past generations, but the available evidence suggests that the gap between approved standards and actual practice has always been considerable. Even the stern preaching of watchful Puritan divines, we are told, proved ineffective in preventing sexual failure among the elect—it merely inhibited the sinner from enjoying his sin.

SOURCES OF DIFFICULTY

One of the immediate sources of the current malaise stems from the fact that we have tended to adjust to social change by adopting new patterns of sexual conduct without duly considering whether the purposes and values they imply are consonant with the broader framework of beliefs and values concerning life, love, marriage and the family that we continue to profess. But adjustments made apart from a wider value frame of reference are aimless and meaningless. In the practical order, adjustments to change constitute programs of action, and rational programs of action are conclusions based on the logical application of relevant principles or premises of values to sets of pertinent social facts. To be sure, changes in our control over the forces of nature have developed so rapidly, adjustments have been required so extensively, and transitory social imbalances have appeared so regularly that it is understandable why many of our contemporaries should regard general readiness to adjust and adapt as a prime requisite of survival. A growing number, particularly among the younger generation, are beginning to suspect that this narrow concern with only immediate, *ad hoc*, segmented adjustments leaves basic questions unasked: "Why adjust?" and "Adjust in terms of what values and goals?"

Sex is a fundamental dimension of human existence. Because of its connections both with man's striving for personal fulfillment and his consequent need to establish satisfactory relationships with others, neither individuals nor societies can long avoid clarifying their stance in its regard. Individuals who attempt to give sex the "silent treatment" eventually discover that it has an uncomfortable way of reasserting itself, especially when it is most ignored. Societies that are unable to achieve general agreement on its nature and purposes soon find that their sexual mores are being determined by the unprincipled in art, literature, advertising and entertainment, who regard sex as a kind of enduring, providential seven-year-itch to be exploited for profit.

Although sex may have different meanings for different people and may come to have different meanings for the same person at different stages of the life-cycle, it is not this quality of relativity that renders human sexuality problematic. Past and present experience indicates that a major source of difficulty in dealing with sex is the tendency to take a partial or topical view of it, to see it in terms of only one of its dimensions, and to value only one of its many aspects. This seemingly endemic inability to view human sexuality as a connected whole perennially inhibits us from reacting to it with balanced, healthy openness. Following a segmented, topical approach, we attempt to deal with early sexuality, premarital and extramarital sexual experiences, marital relations, conjugal love and parenthood as separate items, apart from the wider personal and social context within which they occur and in terms of which their real significance must be assessed.

Closely associated with this tendency among Christians is a conceptual aberration that might be described as the fallacy of misplaced moral concern. This error stems from an exaggerated fear of sexual concupiscence and a misunderstanding of the nature of sin. All responsible Christians, like former President Coolidge's local minister, are "against sin," but moral concern that fails to distinguish sexual sins from their biological expressions and consequently extends the taint of sinfulness to the generative organs or their psycho-physical activities is seriously misdirected. In the Christian tradition it is held that sin consists in the conscious, deliberate decision to act contrary to God's will as the individual understands it. The physical world is not evil, though it may be employed for evil purposes. Considered in themselves, sexual stimulation, pleasure and activity are morally indifferent. It is the deliberate decision to use them contrary to right order that constitutes sin. Thus the attribution of sinfulness to the physical aspects of sex perverts Christian doctrine regarding the nature of sin and fosters the essentially un-Christian attitude that bodily or physical phenomena are morally tainted.

As a result of this "guilt by association" everything relating to human sexuality comes to be regarded as "carnal," "animal," or a manifestation of man's "lower nature." Such a disparaging view of sexuality not only deprives it of meaning and dignity but encourages well-intentioned though unbalanced preachers and others to initiate a "smear campaign" against it in the hope that this will strengthen self-control and dissuade the faithful from overindulgence. Paradoxically, experience shows that this approach accomplishes neither of its purposes, for it deprives sex of none of its power yet destroys its human significance. We do not eliminate reality by denying its existence or giving it a dirty name. Strange as it may seem, when dealing with the subject of sex, many Christians find it difficult to take seriously the fundamental principle of revelation, "Everything created by God is good," and think it through to its logical conclusions.

Because of this tendency to regard everything related to sex as somehow tainted with moral evil, or, at least, as somehow "dirty," "nasty" and peculiarly "carnal," many parents find it difficult to give their children the instruction and guidance needed to help them develop positive Christian attitudes toward their own sexuality and that of others. For the most part, formal educators in school have been reluctant to admit that man even has a reproductive system, though this endowment is not denied in other higher mammals. Religious teachers frequently give the impression that sex cannot be dealt with positively, thus reducing the virtue of chastity to a meaningless negation fenced around by a series of "don'ts." Nor have moral theologians been much more successful in maintaining a balanced approach. As philosopher Josef Piper characterizes their thinking in his book, *Fortitude and Temperance*, "despite all contrary statements of principle, a smoldering subterranean Manichaeism casts suspicion on everything pertaining to physical reproduction as being somehow impure, defiling, and beneath the true dignity of man."

These sources of difficulty in dealing with sex are not mentioned here for the purpose of ridicule. They should serve to remind us that human sexuality is a peculiarly complex, perennially perplexing phenomenon. It is relatively easy to point out inadequacies in past approaches, but such negative criticism may amount to nothing more than mere scapegoating, a convenient form of escapism designed to disguise our present inability to develop a more adequate approach. In all humility we must acknowledge that our own attitudes toward sex are culturally conditioned, that our own views are necessarily colored by personal disposition and past learning experiences, and that our present generation has no valid assurance that its sexual values and insights are wholly consonant with reality. Under these conditions, the best we can do is to strive to develop an ever more adequately Christian understanding of human sexuality in its wholeness and totality.

RELEVANT DIMENSIONS

An adequately comprehensive view of human sexuality implies, among other things, that we keep in balanced focus the physiological facts, their individual and social implications, and their interpreted meaning or significance in a given cultural frame of reference. Human sexuality is a complex phenomenon not only because it includes disjunctive though complementary personal attributes (bisexuality) and consequently couple-centered fulfillment, but also because one of the functions with which it is associated, the bearing and rearing of children, is closely related to group continuity and survival. The quality of being "sexed" has profound implications for both man and society. Sex never appears as a merely biological phenomenon or a psychologically compartmentalized series of acts. It is one element of the total personality, radically conditioned by this totality and the socio-cultural environment within which the individual develops and seeks personal fulfillment.

Granting that we still lack fully satisfactory knowledge regarding some aspects of human sexuality, we can at least make sure that our approach includes all its presently known dimensions. Hence at the risk of becoming tiresomely academic, I would like to begin by briefly recalling some of its major facets. Considered from the viewpoint of the species, sex signifies that human nature, like all higher forms of mammalian life, is expressed disjunctively in male and female. In this sense, sex may be termed a generic disjunctive attribute of the species; "generic" signifies that it is an attribute shared by other species of mammals; while "disjunctive" indicates that the property of being sexed involves the possession of an incomplete though complementary generative system.

Considered from the viewpoint of the individual, sex appears both as a way of being and relating to the world and a way of being and relating to others. As a way of being and relating to the world it is reflected at all levels of the person's activity: psychophysical, psycho-social, and super-personal or spiritual. As a way of being and relating to others it is reflected in the sexually specific, culturally defined statuses and roles in terms of which boys and girls in a given society are trained, and that later determine their relative social positions, accepted areas of action and permitted aspirational goals as participating members of an adult community.

Considered from the viewpoint of society, sex appears as the basis of that primary human community of life and love variously designed to provide for the mutual development and happiness of the couple, the orderly fulfillment of their sexually associated needs, and the adequate recruitment of new members of society through responsible parenthood. Because the individual's reproductive incompleteness involves couple-centered fulfillment; and above all, because the human infant is born utterly helpless, requiring a relatively long period of nurture, protection, training and affective development, some type of family system is found in all known societies. Such systems may differ widely, but they all include some recognized pattern of mating relationship, some form of ceremony or social arrangement assuring public acknowledgement of this relationship, some established procedure to provide needed economic support for the bearing and rearing of children, and some system of kinship designation defining how blood and marriage relatives are related to members of the nuclear family.

Considered in itself as a specifically reproductive attribute of the individual person, sex appears as a unified though complex system containing a number of components that for purposes of analysis may be studied separately. Among the more significant of these are what might be called its biological-constitutional components; that is, the hereditary, congenital and maturational factors reflected in its chromosomal, gonadal, hormonal, internal and external structural qualities, as well as in its characteristic pattern of growth-cycle, mechanisms of arousal, and erotic threshold. These elements are the essential "givens" of sex, setting limits to its adaptability and providing the basis for all subsequent psychosocial conditioning.

Our understanding of human sexuality must also take into consideration its sex-role components; that is, the behavorial patterns and psychological traits typical of each sex in a given socio-cultural setting, and which the individual acquires or develops through social conditioning and learning experience. Closely associated with these are each person's genital-sex object preference, including the sources of genital-sex arousal, the goal and orientation of the genital-sex drive, and the nature of the object and situation within which genital gratification or orgasm occur. Since man's genital-sex object preference is not innate but learned, it admits of a relatively wide variety of expressions.

A further dimension of human sexuality relates to the fact that it involves unique relationships. As we have indicated, the quality of being sexed in the individual person can be understood adequately only in relation to a reciprocal "other" sex; and it is ultimately on the basis of, or in terms of, this mutually complementary relationship that we determine the meaning of sex. More important, mature sexual activity and fulfillment necessarily involves a relationship not merely to things but to persons. The complete sexual act requires intimate union with a sexually complementary "other," and as a potentially life-transmitting process, may involve still another in the person of a child. This inherent orientation to others endows sex with special significance, for these others are persons.

When discussing human sexual activity, therefore, it is necessary to distinguish between sexual behavior and sexual conduct. Behavior signifies objective, concrete activity; for example, the act of intercourse, or the relatively wide variety of actions that Kinsey characterized as "sexual outlets." Conduct signifies activity as seen in its total human context; that is, it includes meaning, and evaluation in terms of values, purposes and normative standards. Following this distinction, it should be obvious that human sexual conduct, as opposed to biological behavior, always includes an inherent moral component. Because the complete sexual act, considered either as couple-centered fulfillment or a potentially life-transmitting transaction, involves interaction between persons and unique interpersonal relationships, any approach to human sexuality that does not take into consideration its moral dimension must be regarded as radically incomplete and essentially inadequate.

Major Systems of Control

The fact that human sexual goal-behavior is not innate or "built-in," that is, that men and women do not inherit a predetermined drive to accomplish specific behavorial goals in their use of sex, further underlines the importance of developing an adequately comprehensive view of human sexuality. Since this view provides the conceptual basis for a society's approved sexual attitudes and practices, we may expect to find considerable cultural diversity in this regard. As a matter of fact, history does indicate that man's sexually associated relationships have been institutionalized in a wide variety of forms. In practice these constitute the culturally determined and accepted sets of obligatory normative relationships centering around the fulfillment of man's basic sexual needs as these are defined by a given human group. We know very little about human sexual patterns prior to written history, and since the essential data appear to be irretrievably lost, continued research is likely to produce little more than conjecture. To be sure, we do have considerable information concerning the various stages of man's evolution as a biological species, but such evidence pertains to his anatomical development and consequently provides no significant information regarding his corresponding social development.

On the other hand, history indicates that all known human societies have maintained some type of normative standards or codes defining the appropriate expressions of sex for their members. If we reflect on the wide variety of beliefs, values, assumptions and practical concerns that must have entered into the formulations of these codes, we will not be surprised to learn that cultures differ greatly in the way they have defined their prohibitions and permissions in this regard. In general, a review of the relevant cross-cultural data available indicates that past societies have followed two fairly well defined, though not mutually exclusive, approaches in formulating their systems of sexual control. The first may be called "society-centered," in the sense that it seeks to regulate only those expressions of sex that are considered potentially harmful to the welfare of the group. Because some control of sex is needed to maintain a society's reproductive, marriage, kinship, social status and ceremonial systems, regulations are formulated and maintained in terms of these systems.

Most cultures developed outside the Jewish and Christian spheres of influence have followed this society-centered approach in developing their sexual codes. Since the general welfare rather than sex itself is the major focus of concern, these codes are designed either to insure social order or secure divine protection. Thus sex relations may be forbidden between certain classes or persons within the kinship group or immediate community, and before or during certain ritual celebrations, group activities or sacred seasons. Beyond these prohibtions, free sexual expression is permitted to the individual. In other words, sexual conduct becomes the object of moral concern only to the extent that it relates to group interests.

The second approach may be termed "person-centered," in the sense that it focuses concern on the individual and his personal responsibility for all voluntary, conscious use of his sexual faculties. Hence it seeks to develop normative standards covering all such expressions of sex under all circumstances. The use of sex in this personalist approach is evaluated primarily in terms of the perfection of the person; and in practice, sexual controls will appear to focus on the sexual faculty itself rather than on those specific expressions of sex that the group may judge to be particularly disruptive of social order. This means that the deliberate, conscious use of sex will be regarded as morally good only to the extent that it conforms to what is believed to constitute the fulfillment of the person's divinely designed nature and destiny.

These two approaches differ significantly inasmuch as the first evaluates sexual conduct in terms of some other social phenomenon in respect to which it is judged important; the second, in terms of a defintie conception of the human person as accountable for all his actions before God. According to the first approach, only those uses of sex that have recognized social significance have moral relevance; according to the second, every willed, conscious use must be morally evaluated; that is, every thought, word and action concerned with sex is held to be regulated by a personally supervised code that is devised with respect to a creator, an integral destiny, and a social purpose. Both approaches lead to the development of a set of culturally standardized practices that range through definitely prescribed, preferred or permitted patterns of conduct to those that are definitely proscribed. With varying degrees of adequacy, both solve the perennial problem of reconciling the need for sexual control with the need for sexual expression; in each approach, however, solutions are developed on the basis of different conceptual starting-points and premises of values.

These two polar approaches must be kept in mind when studying the practical implications of the current "sex revolution." For the most part, the American people, as products of western culture, have tended to follow and take for granted a person-centered approach in formulating their normative sexual standards. It is now becoming increasingly clear that large numbers are beginning to reject or seriously question these standards because they no longer accept the philosophical and theological assumptions upon which this personalist approach was initially founded. At the same time, since they appear either unwilling or incapable of undertaking the logical alternative of developing new sexual standards on the basis of a society-centered approach, the present sexual trend can perhaps best be characterized as a confused, uneasy drift toward normlessness.

RELIGION AND ETHICS

Because most systems of moral values institutionalized in known societies, together with the concepts that give them cognitive meaning, are commonly presumed to be either directly of religious origin or more or less closely related to religious beliefs, there is a tendency to identify religion and ethics, or, at least, to assume a necessary relationship between them. Nevertheless, in the practical order, judgments of value may not be directly related to religious beliefs; while in the speculative order, ethical systems have been developed without explicit religious referents. Although no societies presently known to us are found to be morally indifferent, it is not clear that religious beliefs fulfill a creative function in the formulation of ethical outlooks among all human groups, unless religion is so broadly defined as to be indistinguishable from some kind of ultimate concern.

In other words, religion and ethics are not necessarily interrelated; and what is more important for our present purpose, even the nature of the relationship between a specific religious denomination and the ethical system it develops is far from obvious. A glance at the history of the Christian churches proves enlightening in this regard. Their solutions to the moral issues generated by the industrial revolution, for example, provide little evidence of a direct, consistent relationship between ethics and religious doctrine; while a comparison of Latin American, Continental, and American Catholicism indicates that even Christian communities initially embracing similar religious beliefs may develop considerably different ethical viewpoints and patterns of moral conduct. Thus, although the traditional Christian approach to sex is person-centered and implies a distinctive conception of the human person, his relationship to God, and his consequent moral responsibility, the nature of the relationship between Christian sexual ethics and Christian dogma remains to be explained.

The Founder of Christianity did not present a detailed code of ethics and none will be found in the Gospels. The ethical ideals of purity of heart, a God-centered orientation of life, and readiness to serve God in the Kingdom have a rational aspect and are open to further cognitive development, but the essential dynamic of the Gospel message, which was to work as a leavening force throughout the world, was the command to love—to love God and neighbor—two precepts but one love, as a great Church Father reminds us. As the early Christian communities, although somewhat eschatologically inhibited in the beginning, gradually fashioned their distinctive modalities of creed, cult, and code, their varied cultural predispositions toward developing different doctrinal and ethical emphases became apparent. As a result, the Christian communities of the East came to differ from those in the West, while ethical thought in both tended to develop along two distinct though related lines; that is, in terms of what might be called a "wisdom" morality reserved for a religious elite and a "code" morality for the majority.

History therefore indicates that we may take it as a general principle that the ethical perspectives and normative moral standards associated with a given religion will depend not only on the inherent logic of its doctrinal principles but also upon the sociocultural environment within which they are developed. The relationship between religion and society is a two-way street. The sexual ethics of American Christians necessarily reflect the influence of American society; and I might add, the American experience is so interesting because it represents the point in western history when the churches were disestablished and traditional Christian thought was most completely exposed to the full impact of pluralism and change in an open, democratic society. Under these circumstances, the various religious denominations were forced to re-examine their traditional moral premises and normative standards, for their status as voluntary minority organizations did not permit them to deal with social change by attempting to put new wine into old wineskins under the protective aegis of coercive secular power.

The principle that the ethical system associated with a given religion is profoundly conditioned by the socio-cultural environment within which it develops suggests that the relationship between religious and ethical systems is not direct, but it does not in itself explain the nature of the relationship. Perhaps an analysis of the two systems will throw some light on the problem. Briefly, we may define a system of ethics as a more or less integrated, hierarchically arranged set of general moral principles, together with the complex of related codes and norms representing the culturally defined application of these principles to the various categories of human action routinely encountered by the group. A developed ethical system defines both the morally acceptable ends of human activity and the means by which they are licitly to be achieved. In the final analysis, every ethical system implies a conception or image of man, the human agent. This image includes a set of beliefs regarding man's origin; his relationships to space and time; the essential qualities of his nature and consequently of his orientation to his fellowmen, society, and the world of nature; and finally, his life purpose or destiny, that is, the desirable terminus of his development or fulfillment in the cosmic order as his group defines it. In other words, although all men recognize the quality of oughtness in human conduct, they define the specific contents of this oughtness on the basis of their distinctive image of the human person.

For present purposes, we may define a religious system as the complex of creed, cult, and code constituting a human group's total conception both of their relationships to the transcendent and of the practical consequences thought to stem from these relationships. Hence it includes a set of beliefs regarding a transcendent entity or entities having a significant relationship of supremacy over man and the human condition; a cluster of dogmas, myths and symbols embodying expressions of these beliefs; a cycle of sacred feasts, ceremonies and rites designed to assure doctrinal purity and continuity among the faithful; and a code of conduct covering activities prescribed or proscribed by creed and cult. In other words, it serves to determine the believer's position in the cosmic order by defining his relationships to time, nature, his fellowmen and the divine, and thus answers his basic questions regarding who he is, whence he comes, and what he should strive to become.

Although the clarity and explicitness with which various religious systems answer these questions may differ in degree, they all provide their adherents with the essential components constituting their conception or image of man. Since this image is the ultimate starting point of all ethical systems, the relationship between religion and ethics becomes clear. To the extent that a given religion clarifies the basic components of the conception of man held by its adherents, it furnishes the indispensable ideological foundation for their system of ethics. This all adds up to saying that men develop their definitions of what is right or wrong in the practical order within a broader framework of value referents, organized into fairly consistent schemes or general patterns and related to their conception of man and the world. In addition to the formally prescribed and proscribed activities associated with creed and cult, a religious system affects the ethical judgments of the faithful primarily to the extent that it determines their conception of man.

An adequate understanding of the relationship between religion and ethics involves one further consideration. We must know how the members of a given religious group envisage what might be called the ethical process. A general religious imperative such as the command to love one's neighbor as oneself acquires ethical significance in the practical order only when it is applied to specific human relationships in concrete situations, and there are several possible ways of making this application. For example, one may follow a system of casuistry and seek for precedents or directives in past religious documents regarded either as revealed or as the inspired *dicta* of great religious leaders; one may maintain that because the order of creation was vitiated by the Fall, it no longer reveals the divine plan; so that apart from the limited, explicit directives found in the Bible, the patterns of ethical ideals and normative standards we currently formulate must be regarded as relative, culture-bound products having no essential direct relationship to religious beliefs conceived as absolutes; or finally, one may hold that the Creator's law can be discovered by human reason in the natures of things, and thus the ethical process is considered dynamic and existential in the sense that human reason, aided by insights drawn from revelation and tradition, strives to formulate appropriate patterns of ethical conduct in terms of the changing exigencies of the situation.

The far-reaching significance of different views regarding the ethical process appears most clearly when the churches are confronted with wholly new situations. Although the major religious faiths in America have uniformly assumed that their beliefs had ethical relevance, it is becoming apparent that they are finding it increasingly difficult to demonstrate this relevance particularly in regard to sexual ethics. Because the social and cultural factors affecting sex, love, marriage and the family have been radically modified, the past provides few precedents for dealing with the present, while traditional conceptual frameworks are no longer adequate for developing authentic religious perspectives. This explains why I have judged it useful to begin with a brief overall view of the major dimensions of the problem, for these indicate not only the basic, elemental "givens" relating to human sexuality and its functions but also the diversity, variability, possibilities for rational intervention and consequent "degrees of freedom" associated with these givens as revealed in past sexual experience.

THE CATHOLIC TRADITION

When the Christian religion was introduced into the Hellenic world, the faithful possessed no clearly defined, specifically Christian conceptions of sex, love, marriage and the family. The early Christians lived these realities before they began to theorize about their nature and essential qualities. Whether as Jews or gentiles, they were drawn from long established cultural systems, within which they had been raised, were currently involved, and for the most part continued to live. As a spiritual movement, Christianity did not attempt to destroy or replace these systems; yet its doctrine relating to chastity, the equality of the sexes before God, the value of human life and the sanctity of the marriage bond exerted a gradual leavening influence on the attitudes and practices of all who accepted it.

As the new religion spread, the need to evaluate various alien sexual systems, as well as to refute numerous heretical tendencies among the faithful, forced Church leaders to clarify their thinking and make more explicit the practical implications and profound spiritual insights of the Gospel message in this regard. The conception that finally emerged was a synthesis of Christian, Jewish, Hellenic, Teutonic and other elements that Catholic theologians and canonists had gradually shaped into a fairly consistent system of beliefs, values, principles and practical norms embodying the Church's basic teaching on sex, love, marriage and the family. Yet from the very beginning there appeared those puzzling cross-currents of contradictory sexual theories and attitudes that have continued to inhibit balanced Christian thinking down through the centuries.

For example, we find pre-Augustinian Christian leaders so beset by a rigorism that questioned the inherent goodness or holiness of marriage and a laxity that denied the preeminence of consecrated virginity as a way of life that they remained chiefly preoccupied with the pastoral problem of refuting doctrinal extremes. Augustine's classic definition of the "goods" of marriage could have laid the foundation for a more positive theological approach, but his assumptions regarding sexual concupiscence and original sin prevented this. Briefly, he argued that inasmuch as sexuality in fallen man was vitiated by the most virulent form of concupiscence, *libido carnalis*, the marital act could not be regarded as good in itself but must always be justified by recourse to an external good, namely, the intention to procreate.

Proceeding on this assumption that sexual concupiscence was evil in itself or in its use, Christian thinkers for the next thousand years were primarily concerned either with discovering extrinsic reasons that would justify marital relations or warning married couples against excessive enjoyment even in their legitimate use. Although Thomas Aquinas and later scholastic thinkers added important distinctions concerning the nature and purposes of marriage, their attitudes toward sexual concupiscence remained basically in the Augustinian tradition. Only during the sixteenth and seventeenth centuries do we discover the beginnings of that more balanced counter-current of opinion which would question the adequacy of this pessimistic view and lead to its gradual modification and abandonment.

Two other indications that Christian theologians have experienced great difficulty in developing an objective, adequately integrated view of human sexuality merit mention here because they underline the importance of cultural factors in the formation of ethical concepts. Although conjugal love has always been highly esteemed in the Christian tradition, it has become formally conceptualized as a value meriting special attention from theologians only in relatively recent times. The term *conjugal love* is not univocal, of course, and our conceptions of it, as of all relationships between the sexes, are culturally conditioned and consequently admit of a wide variety of meanings and expressions. In one form or another and in varying degrees of intensity, conjugal love is found and valued in all known societies. As understood in contemporary western society, however, it requires *de facto* as well as *de jure* equality of partners; and since the socio-cultural changes making possible the enhanced status of women are fairly recent, this may partially explain its past relative neglect in theological circles.

In our small, nuclear type family system, moreover, conjugal love has come to play a strategic role in assuring the stability of marriage, and it was undoubtedly their awareness of this fact that led the Council Fathers of Vatican II to assign it a central position in their treatment of marriage.

Further, throughout most of the Christian past there appears little understanding or appreciation of feminine sexuality and even less concern with the wife's enjoyment of marital relations. Though this is usually assumed to be the result of religiously induced feminine prudery or a predominantly male-centered approach to sexuality, such explanations reveal a serious lack of adequate historical and cultural perspective. Given the absence of scientific, medical and obstetrical assistance during both pregnancy and childbirth, and the distressingly high maternal and infant mortality rates characterizing most of the past, together with the lack of any reliable and morally acceptable means of separating marital relations from conception, it should be obvious that women would develop quite different attitudes toward sexual intercourse than men and would consequently tend to regard marital relations primarily as a necessary burden, the prelude to inevitable suffering, sorrow and danger. Under these conditions, it is not surprising to discover that the wife's expression of conjugal love in marital relations came to be regarded as the dutiful proffering of the marriage "debt," an onerous obligation to which society, moral theologians and spiritual directors would devote considerable attention.

At the same time, once knowledge and acceptance of various contraceptive birth control techniques became widespread, religious leaders uniformly reacted by placing primary emphasis on the right use of the marital act as the major criterion for judging its moral quality. Their concern with the negative aspects of the act, a typical example of that doctrinal imbalance that frequently occurs when highly valued moral standards come under attack, while it did not wholly ignore the changing significance of feminine sexuality, tended to leave its positive implications largely unexplored.

With these historical and cultural limitations in mind, let us briefly review the major elements in the traditional Catholic approach to sexual morality. The fundamental premise underlying this approach is that there exists an essential relationship between the use of sex and marriage. To the extent that human sexual activity is the conscious, voluntary act of a responsible person, it can achieve its full value and significance only if it is conjugal, that is, only if it is the expression and actualization of that community of life and love established by the human couple in marriage. On the basis of this premise, Catholic theologians proceeded to develop a fairly comprehensive set of moral principles and norms relating to the right use of sex throughout life.

Two basic concerns have dominated their thinking: first, the protection of human life in any and every form—hence their repeated condemnation of abortion and infanticide; second, respect for "nature," that is, for the meaning or significance of an act as revealed in its objective natural structure—hence their continued insistence on the obligation to respect the integrity of the marital act, and their consequent condemnation of all and various contraceptive techniques. In short, they maintain that any direct, deliberate attempt to inhibit or obstruct the normal structure and progress of the physiological process that a couple freely initiate when engaging in marital relations constitutes an objectively immoral act. Pope Paul recently reiterated this position in his encyclical, *Humanae Vitae*, insisting that the marital act must always be open to procreation.

In their formal treatment of sexual ethics, Catholic theologians usually define chastity as the virtue designed to regulate the use of sex in conformity with right reason. As such, it may be regarded as a form of the cardinal virtue of temperance, the general virtue pertaining to those human appetites having to do with such sentient pleasures as are associated with eating, drinking and touch. According to their view, the chaste person is one who actualizes the order of reason in the use of sex; that is, the order corresponding to the reality made evident to man through both human knowledge and faith. Sins against chastity, therefore, are transgressions or violations of right order in this regard. In sum, they conclude that right order requires that all directly deliberate, voluntary expressions of the sensitive appetite for venereal pleasure must be avoided by the unmarried and used in a manner consonant with the nature of the conjugal vocation and the generative faculties by the married.

The major elements of this teaching went unchallenged for centuries, though the very limited historical evidence presently available suggests that the gap between official teaching and actual practice was probably extensive. The first serious questioning of the adequacy of this approach began around the sixteenth century when a series of developments in science, industry, medicine and travel, together with the introduction of radically new thought-ways in philosophy and theology, began gradually to transform many long accepted western attitudes and practices relating to standards of living, infant and maternal health care, social mobility, the status of women and the formal education of children. Above all, the traditional belief that man should not interfere with his bodily processes or the normal course of life, since generation, birth and death were parts of a providentially ordered cosmic design over which he had no direct dominion, underwent gradual erosion under the impact of mounting secular concern and growing scientific mastery of nature's forces.

The profound implications of these changes were initially ignored by the Church's theologians. Even when it became obvious that the traditional interpretations of sexuality were no longer capable of supplying a meaningful moral framework within which effective ways of meeting the changed exigencies of procreation under contemporary conditions could be developed, both religious and secular leaders were so convinced on *a priori* grounds that family limitation was morally and socially evil that they never bothered to re-examine the assumptions underlying their own positions and strenuously opposed what was happening. As a result of this official rejection, every form of family planning came to be regarded as a deviation, albeit a "culturally patterned" deviation, while numerous adjustments in sexual, marital and family patterns were introduced in an *ad hoc*, piecemeal manner, with little concern for their consonance with the beliefs and values these patterns embodied, and little awareness of their long-range consequences.

During the past few decades, however, a number of Catholic scholars have seriously questioned the adequacy of the Church's sexual ethics. Perhaps the sharpest challenge comes from those who contend that Catholic moral theologians have never objectively confronted human sexuality in its totality; that is, they have never attempted to develop an integrated, logically consistent interpretation of sex, based on an objective analysis of its complex nature and functions as actually reflected in the experience of the species. For the most part, their premises of values and normative conclusions relating to the right use of sex have been formulated piecemeal and in pastoral reaction to various heretical extremes. Thus, although the Church's present corpus of moral doctrine is admittedly the result of the gradual accumulation of principles, norms, and authoritative *dicta* initially developed in the sermons, ascetical writings, and *penitentialia* of the first Christian millenium and later subjected to the rational clarification of scholastic thought, as well as the pragmatic refinements of accommodating casuists, the implicit cultural, scientific, philosophical, theological, and ascetical inadequacies or biases of its original sources have never been carefully examined and hence remain unrecognized and unacknowledged.

The Council Fathers of Vatican II showed that they were well aware of these criticisms and took them seriously. Among other points, they recognized the implications of current population trends, acknowledged the need for some form of family regulation, stressed the necessity of up-grading the education and social participation of women, and displayed a mature understanding of the sexual dimensions of conjugal love. Considering the long and troubled history of Christian attempts to discover the Creator's plan in regard to sex and marital relations, this latter point may be regarded as one of the Council's most significant contributions in pastoral theology. Thus after pointing out that conjugal love is "eminently human" and "involves the good of the whole person," it declares, "Therefore, it can enrich the expressions of body and mind with a unique dignity, ennobling these expressions as special ingredients and signs of the friendship distinctive of marriage. This love the Lord has judged worthy of special gifts, healing, perfecting, and exalting gifts of grace and charity." And lest there be any lingering doubts concerning the goodness of sexual relations in marriage, the Council adds, "This love is uniquely expressed and perfected through the marital act. The actions within marriage by which the couple are united intimately and chastely are noble and worthy ones. Expressed in a manner which is truly human, these actions signify and promote that mutual self-giving by which spouses enrich each other with a joyful and a thankful will."

To my knowledge, these statements are unique among the Church's official documents on sex and marriage. They do not solve all the delicate, intimate personal problems involved in achieving mature sexual adjustment in marriage, but by assigning marital relations a central role in the normal expressions of conjugal love and attributing special unifying properties to these expressions, they furnish a sound basis for a balanced Christian orientation to such problems and to human sexual relations in general.

For reasons that he did not make clear, Pope Paul did not see fit to follow the Council's teaching on this point when formulating his solution to the problem of family regulation. As a matter of fact, it would not be easy to reconcile the two positions. The Pope's restatement of the Church's long-standing condemnation of contraceptive birth control is based on an analysis of marital relations as a potentially life-transmitting transaction, the essential structure of which must always be respected since it signifies the Creator's intent. On the other hand, following the Council's statements, one must conclude that if the affective fulfillment resulting from the ongoing sexual exchange built into the very intimacy of the marriage state has health-giving qualities highly significant for the maintenance of conjugal love, marital stability, companionship and communication, the observance of absolute or relatively prolonged continence may seriously jeopardize the essential "goods" of marriage (*fides, proles, sacramentum*).

Despite the air of ambiguity currently characterizing the Church's official teaching regarding marital relations, it should be observed that this marks only the initial stage of a long overdue critical reappraisal of the specifically Catholic approach to human sexuality. From the beginning, the Church's teaching in this regard constituted an attempt to define, foster and protect basic values relating to sex, love, marriage and the family as these values were currently understood. This aim must remain paramount. What the present reappraisal involves is the careful reformulation of these values in the light of contemporary cultural and theological developments, together with a searching reassessment of the normative means formerly judged necessary to assure their attainment.

In other words, our present understanding and appreciation of sex and marriage are the result of a long historical development characterized by marked changes in the family system and consequently in the statuses and roles of family members; by extensive scientific advances in our knowledge of man's generative faculties and sexual behavior; and by new theological insights regarding the inherent dignity of the human person and the meaning of the Christian's vocation in the present economy of salvation. Thus the unique human significance and value of conjugal love; the specially unifying, affective, relational importance of sexual relations in expressing and fostering this love; and the crucial, greatly expanded function of parenthood under contemporary conditions are gradually emerging into clearer Christian perspective and must now be fully integrated into the Church's total conception of human sexuality.

Because the mature full use of sex necessarily involves a relationship not to things but to persons, serious Christians are rightfully concerned with exploring and clarifying its morally acceptable expressions within their constantly evolving cultural contexts. A responsible judgment in this regard must be grounded on a balanced consideration of the functions that sex is designed to serve in promoting the integral development and fulfillment of the human person throughout the life-cycle. Human experience, revelation and reason strongly suggest that since sexual relations are designed both to unite the partners in a mysterious two-in-one-flesh solidarity as persons and to provide for the continuity of the race through parenthood, sex can be used responsibly only by married couples; that is, only by a man and woman who have irrevocably committed themselves to maintan an exclusive community of love and life within which they can strive for mutual happiness and fulfillment and thus create the human environment within which children can be fittingly reared.

This high aim, combining sex, love and shared responsibility, remains an ideal to be attained. Men and women are not endowed with a sex instinct innately directing their sexual behavior toward clearly defined goals; nor do human sexual relations automatically become expressions of love, for sex can be used to express a wide range of emotions and to achieve a variety of purposes. The human attribute of sex merely endows the individual with the potential capacity of becoming sexually mature and relating to a partner in a loving, uniquely fulfilling, mutually responsible way.

At the present time, Catholic thinkers are beginning to tackle the difficult task of reappraising the conceptual framework of beliefs, value premises, attitudes and assumptions within which their distinctive sexual ethics historically developed. Like most religious leaders in the western world, they have long failed to understand the radical implications of the socio-cultural changes that have been profoundly reshaping modern man's conceptions of sex, love, marriage and the family. Under the circumstances, we must not be surprised if their efforts to cleanse the Church's essential gospel message of its accumulated cultural accretions and render it relevant to our present human condition will reflect some uncertainty, confusion, conflicting viewpoints and controversy. This is perhaps inevitable, but need not be exaggerated. If we may hazard a prediction, the major result of the current reappraisal will be to place greater personal responsibility on marriage partners and require that they mutually foster an ever deepening awareness of both the natural and supernatural dimensions of the vocation they have chosen as their personal way of loving God and neighbor.

8

Sexual Ethics in Christian Tradition

•

DERRICK SHERWIN BAILEY

Famed for his studies in biblical theology and sexual relationship, D.S. Bailey here compiles the volume's historical overview of
sexual ethics in the Christian tradition. Dr. Bailey is precentor at
Wells Cathedral, England. His books include *The Mystery of Love
and Marriage, Homosexuality and the Western Christian Tradition,
Sexual Offenders and Social Punishment, Sexual Relation In Christian Thought,* and *Common Sense About Sexual Ethics.*

BY RACE AND CULTURE the first Christians were Jews, Greeks and Romans who brought with them into their new faith some at least of their traditional ideas about sex. They continued to share with their pagan contemporaries certain assumptions and attitudes about marriage, woman and sexual status and relation which were almost universally current in antiquity; and they stood under a common civil law which defined the position of woman and regulated the formation of marriage. The Jewish respect for marriage and the family was continued in the Christian ideal of the home as in some sense a 'religious institution' in which natural relationships were elevated and strengthened through the sharing of a common faith and the practice of charity. Hellenistic influences were on the whole negative: the license of the times and the moral laxity of pagan religion engendered an almost puritanical attitude toward sexual relation and coition, and this was reinforced by the ascetical ideals of philosophy and a rigoristic strain in some of the mystery cults which combined to create a climate of opinion which tended to associate the pursuit of true religion with mortification and particularly the practice of sexual continence.

But the Christian sexual tradition did not originate only in a fusion of Jewish and Hellenistic ideas. Jeus himself did not proclaim any new sexual ethic, but simply recalled his hearers to the first principles of sex and sexual relation inherent in God's creative purpose. His insistence upon these principles, however, and upon the duty of love and forgiveness, meant that from the first certain truths were recognized as part of the Gospel—the spiritual equality of the sexes before God, the high theological significance of marriage, and the impartial application of the rule of chastity to men and women alike. The original element in the Christian sexual tradition was a different and higher conception of Man than

that taught by the philosophers, and the conviction that in Christ
a new life was offered through the Holy Spirit, capable of redeem-
ing and transforming man and woman in their relationships. But
the radical implications of this were not quickly or easily perceived
—and when they were, they often seemed dangerous.

The writings of St. Paul had a more directly formative influence
upon the Christian sexual ethic, but this influence has often been
wrongly evaluated. He was unmistakably a child of his time, at-
tracted to the ascetical notions which were in the air, convinced
that the end of the ages was at hand—and probably temperamentally averse from marriage. Yet he shows himself a wise and realistic pastor as he interprets the freedom and obligations of the
Gospel to those who were living in a world which seemed to be
nearing its close. Though we cannot accept his view that marriage
is a necessary concession to human frailty ('it is better to marry
than to burn'), and that only the unmarried show a true concern
for the things of God, we can readily endorse his teaching that
coition is an act which engages and expresses the whole personality, and a right of which husband or wife must not defraud one
another. He sees marriage as a "great mystery" symbolizing the
union of Christ and the Church—an idea which transforms the
while spirit of marriage in the ancient world; yet the husband is
still the 'head' of the wife, and woman was created for the benefit
of man. This want of consistency in St. Paul's thought reveals a
tension in early Christian ethical thought between progressive and
reactionary elements which was eventually eased but never wholly
resolved as eschatological expectations receded and Christians adjusted themselves to the conditions of every-day life.

From St. Paul's assertion that the unmarried care for the things
of God, but the married for those of the world, the early Church
drew the conclusion that in the pursuit of Christian perfection
abstinence from coition was the critical discipline. A cult of virginity was promoted, and the celibate state was commended as
higher than marriage—by some, such as Tertullian and Jerome,
fanatically; by others more temperately. Little support or sympathy
was accorded to the few who protested against what seemed to

them a dangerous abuse. But this predilection for virginity set a theological problem. Marriage and all that belonged to it were clearly good gifts by God to Man, and nothing must be conceded to heretical elements which maintained that they were evil and impure. An answer was found in the theory that marriage, though inferior to virginity, was none the less a secondary good with its distinctive blessings of children, mutual fidelity, and sacred symbolism—but for all this, still a concession to human frailty; if they could not condemn it, the early Fathers would not commend it, and were never weary of drawing attention to its trials and disadvantages. Whatever Scriptural authority was adduced for this exaltation of virginity, there can be no doubt that it was not Christian in origin, but had its roots in the Hellenistic and Oriental dualism which regarded the material things of life and the world as intrinsically evil, and only those of the spirit as good.

THE CHURCH FATHERS

It is clear that this attitude to marriage was chiefly due to the unconcealed antipathy of the Fathers to coition. Some of them saw no essential difference between marriage and fornication, since in both cases the same act was performed, and all tended to treat marriage principally if not exclusively in terms of its procreative function. Although the begetting of children was held to be good, the means which God had appointed for this purpose were sometimes deplored, and Augustine and others commended those who lived continently in marriage and left to pagans the mundane and somewhat sordid business of continuing the race.

Only Augustine, however, attempted a theological estimate of coition, though there is no doubt that he spoke for all. He was much embarrassed by the manner in which coition is accomplished, and by the intensity of the emotions which precede and accompany the act. He could not believe that God had intended Man to procreate in this way, and so attributed coition, as now experienced, to the Fall. He did not assert that the first sin was sexual; rather, the Fall caused Adam and Eve to seek self-satisfaction at all costs and at the expense of every other good. This disposition he termed concupiscence, and he held that concupiscence weakened Man's rational control of his nature. From the involuntary character of sexual excitement and the uncontrollability of the orgasm he further deduced that concupiscence, though present in all our members, was located particularly in our sexuality—with the result that he arrived at a practical equation of original sin, concupiscence, and sexual emotion from which he inferred that coition, though good in theory (being ordained to a good end, procreation), was in practice intrinsically evil.

The purpose of marriage, then, is to procure forgiveness for coition by directing concupiscence to a good end and transforming the satisfaction of lust into a necessary duty, so excusing the inherent sinfulness of the act. If procreation is its only motive, God accounts it blameless, but if the motive is alleviation of desire, coition is only sinful to a slight degree within marriage; outside marriage, coition is always mortally sinful. Finally, while an intention to procreate relieves coition between the married of sin, the act remains a channel through which concupiscence is transmitted to the child; hence the need for baptismal regeneration in which the guilt of concupiscence is washed away, though the impulse remains. This theory was modified by Gregory the Great, who found the evil element in coition, not in concupiscence but in sexual pleasure; and it exerted a profound influence upon all subsequent sexual ideas, both in the Church and in the whole western Christian culture.

The status of the sexes is never without ethical significance, and here the early Christian attitude was ambiguous. The theological principle of the spiritual equality of the sexes did not find expression in a corresponding social and matrimonial equality, and although woman was treated with a new respect, her legal position remained unchanged. Moreover, she had to bear the reproach of Eve's transgression, mitigated though this was by admission that redemption no less than sin came through a woman. Patristic misogyny, though rationalized by reference to the Fall, was to some extent rooted in the antipathy to physical sexuality already mentioned; woman was also weak, unstable, frivolous, and a dangerous temptress! We note, too, a regression from the single moral standard inculcated at the first; by the fourth century in the East opinion was more lenient towards an adulterous husband than towards an adulterous wife.

Despite one or two obscure references, there is no doubt that the Church's prohibition of divorce absolute was applied with the strictest consistency during the first Christian centuries. Separation was allowed in extreme cases, but forgiveness and resumption of cohabitation were inculcated. It was again Augustine who elucidated the theology of the matrimonial bond. He held that the bond consisted of an enduring moral obligation which only death could cancel—an obligation, unaffected by separtion, to reserve the right of coition for the marriage partner alone. The bond was thus not spiritual or metaphysical, even though in separation there remained between the spouses what Augustine termed 'a certain element of conjugality'; marriage was not indissoluble in the sense of ontologically unbreakable, but it ought not to be broken because of the coital obligation which it set up. Further, the formal unity of marriage ought to be maintained in order to preserve intact the 'sacrament' or symbolism of marriage as a sign of the union of Christ and the Church, of the Incarnation, and so forth. Separation might mar this symbolism, but only death could destroy it.

The sacramental idea of marriage presented a high ideal of the union, even though it was regarded as inferior to virginity and widowhood. In other ways Christian thought contributed to a higher view of marriage than that generally current in antiquity —for instance, by insisting upon the moral obligation of permanence, and by permitting unions (such as those of slaves and free women, approved by Pope Callistus) which were deemed invalid by the state, though in no way contrary to divine law. But any final estimate of the early Christian view of marriage and sexual ethics cannot overlook the all-pervading influence of dualistic ideas of sex derived from Hellenism and the East, though it must not be allowed to obscure the more positive aspects—such as a new regard for the sanctity of human life which showed itself in condemnation of abortion and the exposure of children, and the requirement from believers of a standard of sexual behaviour which contrasted markedly with the licentiousness of contemporary society.

The Church condemned homosexual as well as heterosexual immorality. Early Christian attitudes to male homosexualism (for female practices were ignored) were moulded partly by biblical denunciations of unnatural behaviour and partly by the Roman law. The Christian emperors continued to enforce the statutes of their precedessors, and the Theodosian Code prescribed the penalty of death by burning; but Justinian, who was the first to invoke the 'homosexual' interpretation of the Sodom story, was concerned less to punish offenders than to bring them to repentance, and legal penalities were reserved for the obdurate. In contrast to the legislators, early Christian moralists and disciplinary rules do not regard homosexualism as deserving of exemplary punishment, though they regard it as gravely sinful.

THE MIDDLE AGES

During the Middle Ages Christian treatment of questions of sexual ethics was fuller and more systematic, due mainly to the Church's greater official concern with the legal and social aspects of marriage and sexual relationship. Social and political circumstances served to focus interest first upon divorce and remarriage, for Frankish and German converts imported into the Church north of the Alps a liberal tradition which royalty and nobility continued to invoke, while the disruption and uncertainty of life in the Dark Ages caused doubt about unions long broken by the accidents of the times. Several celebrated divorce cases gave Rome an opportunity to declare without compromise that marriage is permanent until the intervention of death. On the other hand, Archbishop Theodore of Canterbury, an Easterner who introduced into England some of the permissiveness of the Byzantine Church, departed from this strict rule in cases of capture, abduction, and presumptive death due to war and similar contingencies, and his concessions found their way into some of the continental Church law books. The reforms of Gregory VII, however, restored the stricter practice of earlier times.

It was thus settled that lawful consummated Christian marriage is absolutely indissoluble. Marriage was not, however, held to be indissoluble in natural law. This was partly because it was believed, but mistakenly, that St. Paul had permitted remarriage to a Christian convert deserted by a pagan partner—the so-called 'Pauline privilege,' and partly because being sacramental, Christian marriage had a more enduring character than pagan marriage (though a certain kind of permanence was ascribed to the latter).

During the Middle Ages a new theory of the sacrament of marriage gained acceptance and took precedence over that enunciated by Augustine. According to this theory marriage, though still possessing its symbolism, was sacramental in the sense that it was one of seven efficacious signs expressly instituted by Christ as means by which sanctifying grace is conveyed to the believer. Since natural marriage did not partake of the character of Christ's union with the Church, it could not possess that union's inviolability. Thus Augustine's view of marriage as involving an imperative moral obligation to preserve its permanence was replaced by the idea that it created a metaphysical bond which was indestructible, independently of the moral purpose of the spouses. Marriage no longer ought not to be broken; it could not be broken.

This character of indissolubility attached to Christian marriage depended, however, upon the union being lawful and consummated—and endured until death; one of the large flaws in the whole idea was this qualification, for if marriage was held to effect something in the metaphysical realm, the incidence of death could be argued to be irrelevant. The formation of marriage was a matter which long occupied theologians and canonists, but the discussion was finally closed by a decision of Pope Alexander III that to establish a lawful union nothing was more necessary than the exchange by the couple of free and valid consent in words of present import (*verba de praesenti*). Consent was lawful if it was not impeded by certain restrictions and prohibitions. These forbade the marriage of those closely related by blood or by affinity, and additional bars were created by illicit coition and by sponsorship at baptism or confirmation. The former of these bars was based on the assumption that since coition makes man and woman one flesh, fornication sets up the same impediments to marriage as those brought about by a regular union. The latter had its origin in the theory that sponsorship established a quasi-parental relationship which precluded the subsequent marriage of a godparent with the person baptized, with that person's parents, and with any co-sponsor. By this scheme of impediments many grounds were established on which a marriage could be forbidden or nullified; thus a 'safety-valve' was created which to some extent compensated for the strict refusal of remarriage after divorce—though the annulment of marriages by the ecclesiastical courts was not entirely the abuse that some have claimed it to be.

By accepting the Roman law principle that consent alone effects a marriage the mediaeval Church implicitly endorsed the corollary that coition is an accidental and not an essential element in marriage. This was a conclusion to which Christian thought had long been moving. It facilitated the business of the ecclesiastical courts, since consent has normally a greater evidential value than coition, but underlying the forensic reason there was certainly, as we have already noted, an emotional factor favourable to any idea of marriage which minimized the importance of coition—without which, as Peter Lombard said, marriage is holier. Yet Scripture forbade an absolute rejection of coition: hence the anomalous position that although consent was held to effect a union possessing everything necessary to complete marriage, consummation was still regarded as essential for conferring indissolubility—a contradiction which was never resolved.

The mediaeval view of physical sexuality, however, was on the whole free from the emotional prejudices of the many of the early Fathers, though coition was still a source of some theological embarrassment. Debating its morality, the Scholastics perceived that it was important to preserve a clear distinction between sin and evil. Peter Lombard suggested and Aquinas developed the idea that coition, at first wholly good, had been corrupted by the Fall.

Man's lapse into sin had weakened his will and loosened the rational control which he should ideally exert over all his members and actions, and this defect was particularly evident in the sexual realm; Man cannot now bring his sexuality under full control, and the orgasm especially subordinates the will completely to the emotions—and this is an evil. Thus the evil element in coition is located, not in the act itself, nor in the motivating concupiscence, nor yet in the attendant pleasure, but simply in what Aquinas regarded as the essential irrationality of the act. But for this defect husband and wife were not morally responsible, and within marriage coition was not sinful.

During the Middle Ages Christian thinkers made the first serious attempt to consider the morality, not only of coition, but of sexual acts in general. In the manuals of discipline called Penitentials, compiled for the guidance of confessors, there were sections dealing with sexual offences of all kinds, but it is again to Aquinas that we must turn for a methodical treatment of the matter. He lays down a triple standard for the moral evaluations of sexual acts: they must be done for the right purpose, with the right person, and in the right way. Since the purpose of the genital organs is generation, any exclusion of the possibility of conception is sinful—and this can occur (in ascending order of gravity) in masturbation, coition in a manner unnatural or unbecoming in human beings, beastiality, and homosexualism. Less serious is coition with the wrong person, as in seduction or rape (when the woman is under her father's authority), adultery (when she is under that of her husband), and incest—and in the first two instances an important element in the offence is the infringement of another man's rights. Simple fornication, without any infringement of another's rights, is a venial transgression, unless a child is conceived, when the offence becomes one of those against nature (since the child will lack a father's care and will suffer the stigma of illegitimacy), and correspondingly grave. Kisses, touches and caresses are only sinful if inspired by a wrong motive such as enjoyment of a forbidden pleasure.

Prostitution presented the patristic and mediaeval moralist with a difficult problem; it was to be condemned as sinful, yet in the present condition of society it seemed both unavoidable and in a sense necessary. Even a palace must have sewers, and to abolish prostitution would be to invite an increase in adultery and homosexualism. It was concluded that this was an illustration of a principle observable in God's ordering of the world: that certain ills must be tolerated because they prevented the occurrence of worse ills; prostitution, therefore, is the price that society must pay for the preservation of social purity and feminine chastity. The assumption which went unquestioned was that regular coition is a necessity for every man, and that continence is normally impossible.

Conformable to Aquinas's classification, homosexualism was regarded as a grave sin. Earlier, it had figured in the Penitentials, which deal with the matter comprehensively, distinguishing between male and female practices and between different kinds of acts. In general, the Middle Ages regarded homosexualism as a sin cognizable by the Church; spiritual penalties were imposed, but offenders were rarely surrendered to the civil magistrate for the punishment prescribed by the law, which was often capital. When they were handed over, it was usually for other offences committed in addition to the practice of homosexuality.

While it is clear that towards the end of the Middle Ages moralists were prepared to allow other legitimate ends of coition, so long as the act's procreative purpose was not impeded, there is no indication of any approval for such methods of contraception as were practised at the time. Such methods would undoubtedly come within Aquinas's category of coition in a manner unnatural or unbecoming in human beings.

The calmer and more rational attitude of the Scholastics towards sexual matters is also to be seen in their view of woman and her status. Their thought was just as androcentric as that of the patristic age, but they express themselves more temperately and without emotional prejudice. Woman was destined for social union with man, yet she was not created to be his partner in all the affairs and enterprises of human life, but only in the business of generation. Man is ontologically the superior; Aristotle's anthropology is still dominant—the male is the perfect human being, and the female a deviation from the norm. The persistence of this estimate of woman could not but have serious ethical consequences.

THE REFORMATION

The Reformers of the sixteenth century paid less attention than their mediaeval predecessors to matrimonial and sexual questions, and were generally content rather to correct abuses in the existing system than to re-direct the course of Christian thought on sexual matters. Not only did their predilection for appeals to Scripture conduce to conservatism, but their emotional attitudes, particularly to physical sexuality, were not greatly dissimilar from those of the Schoolmen.

The attack of the Reformers was mounted chiefly against clerical celibacy and obligatory vows of continence, and most of the Confessions and Formularies proclaim the honesty of marriage and the evil of irrevocable monastic vows. Luther strongly attacked the delusion, as he saw it, that God's favour can be won by self-imposed disciplines which imply that salvation is by works and not faith. Continence, he held, is as little in our power as are the rest of the divine graces; all are made for marriage, and sexual desire cannot be restrained by ecclesiastical rules; temptation of God inevitably brings its own reward in uncleanness of living, for which marriage is the appointed remedy. Calvin, here as elsewhere, was more moderate and cautious; he did not condemn monastic vows outright, but only those taken irresponsibly. Like Luther, he denounced the imposition of compulsory celibacy upon the clergy. The two Reformers were divided upon the question of the intrinsic merit of virginity; Luther regarded it as something to be shunned as unnatural, while Calvin held that it is essentially superior to marriage and if undertaken voluntarily should not be despised.

Luther's sexual thought is a curious mixture of radical and conservative elements. He expressed himself eulogistically about marriage: it is God's gift to Man—a heavenly and spiritual state, a school of faith and love in which every menial task, every trouble and hardship, is a means of religious education. Luther was one of the first to perceive in the common life of marriage a true means of sanctification, and one of his greatest contributions to thought in this field was his elevation of that common life to a spiritual level. Yet for him no less than for his predecessors, the sexual impulse and its expression were stumbling-blocks. Like them, he discerned in the sexual relationship the effect of the Fall. Coition, he held, was always attended by a sense of shame, due to loss of trust in God, and is always unclean; yet for most men (and his approach is usually from the male angle) it remains a regrettable but imperative necessity. Hence, despite his eulogy of marriage, he did not hesitate to describe it as a 'medicine' and a 'hospital for the sick'—the only effective antidote to the incontinence that troubles all men.

Calvin, on the other hand, was more positive and less obsessed with physical sexuality. Coition, for him, was holy and had been disparaged as unclean only because Satan has warped Man's judgement and sense of values by representing as evil what is really good. Yet even Calvin could not break entirely with the past, and expressed some uneasiness on account of coital pleasure and desire, which are now (he thought) immoderate in Man because of the Fall—so that while God allows husband and wife to enjoy themselves sexually, he gives them no licence to indulge intemperately. Calvin regarded marriage as a high calling and spared its detractors no denunciation. Though he did not expend upon it the laudation bestowed by Luther, his conception of marriage was more original. He did not deny that children are a characteristic end of marriage, yet he taught that its primary purpose was rather social than procreative. Woman was ordained, not simply to be the companion of man's bed or his partner in the home, but rather his inseparable associate in the whole of life; she was more than a bearer of offspring or a remedy against sin. None the less, like Luther, Calvin accepted the principle of woman's subordinate status, and saw her specific ministry in the Church in terms of motherhood.

While Calvin regarded polygyny as repugnant to God's ordinance and would not even defend the plural unions of the Old Testament patriarchs, Luther (more strongly swayed by sexual considerations) somewhat reluctantly conceded in several cases that bigamy was justified. In so doing he was not arrogating to himself any dispensatory right, but simply stating what (in his view) the law of God allowed in specific cases of conscience. For him, marriage as a social institution was essentially a secular, civil matter, subject to the jurisdiction of the magistrate—who in turn stood under the laws of God and reason. Calvin likewise conceded to the secular authority all matrimonial jurisdiction, but since (unlike Luther) he conceived the state as a theocracy, the Church retained in effect a determining control upon the administration of the law.

Luther and Calvin both rejected the mediaeval idea of the indissolubility of marriage and allowed divorce absolute with a right of remarriage for adultery and for desertion of various kinds, though Lutheran divines found it difficult to halt short of the liberal provisions of the Roman-Byzantine law, while the Calvinists adhered closer to what they believed the New Testament authorized. While both systems thus allowed greater facility for the dissolution of marriage, they drastically simplified the complex scheme of impediments which governed mediaeval practice and rejected the bars arising from illicit coition and spiritual affinity, thus greatly reducing the volume of annulments of marriage and the attendant abuses.

The chief positive contribution of the continental Reformation to sexual ethics was probably its rejection of the ancient double ethical standard which exalted virginity and depreciated marriage. In other respects its achievement was negative—for instance, in rejecting the mediaeval conception of the sacrament of matrimony but failing to revive and elaborate the Augustinian idea of moral obligation, and in permitting greater facilities for divorce and remarriage while leaving unexplored the nature of marriage as a permanent union; and retrogressive tendencies can be discerned. Despite the value set by the Reformers upon home and children, their inculcation of a Semitic ideal of domesticity based upon Old Testament models tended to emphasize the androcentricity of society and the subordination of woman, and established the father of the family in a quasi-magisterial role while stringently subjecting children to a rigorous parental government.

There is also more than a trace of 'puritanism,' not only in Reformed attitudes to sexual matters, but in Counter-Reformation attitudes also. Prudishness was not confined to the Protestants, as we note from the mutilation of Michelangelo's Sistine Chapel nudes. Both sides were probably in their different ways reacting against the liberalism of the Renaissance, and beneath the political and religious divisions of the Reformation there undoubtedly lay common sexual ideas and attitudes which were too deeply ingrained to be easily changed.

THE ANGLICANS

From the point of view of sexual ethics the seventeenth century is more important than the sixteenth in the Anglican Reformation. The evidence, however, is less consistent. Anglican divines show a marked appreciation of the married state and of the value of sexual love, and their conventional assertions of woman's subordinate status are often contradicted by arguments to the contrary, as well as by independent evidence of contemporary woman's actual position. Similarly, the relationship between parents and children is depicted in paternalistic and authoritarian terms, but there are also many signs that a new attitude towards home and the child were beginning to emerge. All this indicates that the typically empirical method of Anglican theology was taking constructive account of the experience of a married clergy.

Tradition had always regarded procreation as the first purpose of marriage, though Luther, as we have seen, laid special emphasis upon the relief of incontinence. The Anglican marriage service also appears to endorse this in its first and second 'causes' for the ordinance of matrimony, but in fact the majority of theologians of the time treat mutual society, help and comfort as the principal purpose of marriage. Again, tradition had always assumed that coition had but one purpose: generation, but Jeremy Taylor shows a new awareness of its relational value when he says that it is also for lightening domestic cares and for mutual endearment.

Regarding the morality of sexual acts in general, Taylor departs from the strict classification of crimes against nature proposed by Aquinas; he holds that such acts are not in themselves worse than any other sins—and not always or necessarily worse than adultery or fornication. They ought not to be assessed by a fixed scale, but motive, occasion and consequence should be taken into account. Taylor also rejected the view of prostitution advanced by Augustine and Aquinas and maintained, with modifications, by later Roman Catholic moralists. This is not, he says, an evil which must be endured for fear that worse may befall; the idea that it is unavoidable is simply an invention to justify its continuance.

In the matter of divorce and remarriage there have always been two strands in Anglican thought, one rigorist and the other liberal. There are signs that some of the more extreme Reformers would have liked a wide permission of divorce absolute on Lutheran lines, but their views never influenced Anglican theory or practice— though a much larger body of opinion favoured the teaching that adultery dissolved the marriage bond. Separation alone was permitted by canon law, but the wealthy and influential could obtain divorce by Act of Parliament at the cost of a financial penalty; some held that the relevant canon proclaimed (or was intended to proclaim) that marriage is indissoluble, while others thought that its purpose was simply to prevent collusion and to check divorce. Certainly there were those who maintained that marriage is indissoluble in the mediaeval sense, but there were also theologians of standing who appear to have revived the Augustinian doctrine of the marriage bond as one of imperative moral obligation—notably Thorndike and Hammond.

Perhaps one of the most important contributions to the theory of marriage made in the seventeenth century was that the doctrine of indissolubility as developed in the Middle Ages was simply a metaphysical figment wholly unrelated to the realities of the situation. On the contrary, several divines maintained that cohabitation—the common life of husband and wife at bed and board—is of the essence of marriage, so that with the permanent disruption of this common life the marriage itself had gone out of existence. This perception that marriage is above all a personal relationship has implications for the Christian attitude to divorce and remarriage which have not yet been fully explored.

SUMMARY

This chapter does no more than summarize in the briefest possible manner the ethical importance of the main features of the Christian sexual tradition.[1] Running through the centuries we note several persistent features—a negative attitude to physical sexuality which infiltrated Christian thought from Hebrew speculation upon the Fall and sin, from the ascetical idealism of Greek philosophy, and from oriental dualism; a double ethical standard which set virginity above marriage and consequently identified the pursuit of the good life partly with sexual asceticism; and a male-centredness which combined with these factors to produce a relatively low view of marriage. We have also noted two qualifying features. First, there was a consistent stress upon a single standard of sexual morality applicable to men no less than to women, and the honesty and integrity of marriage was defended and its permanence maintained. Second, the Christian sexual tradition was a living and growing thing, taking its colour from its successive cultural contexts, yet bearing witness to the new spirit which Christianity gradually infused into marriage and sexual relationship.

In the past, ethical ideas in the sexual field (as we have seen) changed slowly, and some have persisted with only slight modification while others, repudiated by theologians, have become so deeply embedded in our culture that they continue to influence at least popular attitudes, and defy eradication. But during the last

[1] For an expanded treatment of the subject, see D.S. Bailey, *Common Sense about Sexual Ethics*, Macmillan, New York, 1962, or *Sexual Ethics*, Macmillan (Paperback), New York, 1963. For a fully detailed and documented account, see D.S. Bailey, *Sexual Relation in Christian Thought*, Harper & Brothers, New York, 1959 and D.S. Bailey, *Homosexuality and the Western Christian Tradition*, Longmans, Green & Co. Inc., London and New York, 1955.

hundred years many new factors—social and cultural, scientific, psychological and philosophical—have come to bear upon the Christian ethical tradition, and Christianity in turn has shown that it has the theological resources to gain, under the guidance of the Holy Spirit, new and important insights into the nature of human sexuality and the relations of man and woman. The Christian sexual ethic is no fossilized or antiquated survival from the past, significant only on account of its baneful but happily diminishing influence; it is an ethic which is being remoulded in the twentieth century as it was in the seventeenth and the thirteenth centuries, in order that the will of God for contemporary men and women may be more clearly known and more faithfully followed.

9

Sexuality as Celebration and Concern

•

ROBERT H. BONTHIUS

Churches in recent years have made a renewed attempt to relate creed and ethic regarding sexual morality. Dr. Bonthius' United Presbyterian denomination is such a church; and here he describes that attempt in *The Confession of 1967*. Dr. Bonthius is director of the Internship for Clergymen in Urban Ministry at Case Western Reserve University and author of *Christian Paths to Self-Acceptance, The Independent Study Program in the United States,* and *Introduction to the Study of The Bible.*

SEXUALITY IN ITS FULLNESS is a problem for contemporary man, The Kinsey reports have shown us conclusively that overt sexual activity, biologically interpreted, is widespread, in contradiction to civil law and moral standards. The incidence of premarital intercourse and extramarital intercourse is high. Love relations are the most trying and taxing of all relationships. Marriage, the most demanding form of love relations, is not a success for many people. One marriage in every four fails completely. Many more are not love relations but cold wars.

It would be easy to keep on quoting facts that dramatize the inability of our society to realize the promise of marriage or the satisfactions of sexuality. But perhaps one more statistic will do. One out of three teenage marriages is a forced marriage, brought about by unwanted pregnancy. Ask any parent—we have not found the ways in our society to teach ourselves or our children how to love wisely and well.

We are compelled to assess our complicity in this widespread inability to master the complexities of love and sex. As I see it, there are five forms of guilt in this regard. First, and most obvious to people outside this country, is our extremism with regard to sex. I don't know whether it is really true that the Europeans know better how to handle liquor than Americans. I'm not at all sure that they know better how to handle sex than we do. But one has the impression that with sex, as with liquor, Americans have to go to one extreme or the other. It seems to be all or nothing at all. This Puritanism and its opposite, libertinism, this preoccupation with sex, by the moralists who shun it, by the sensualists who think of nothing else—this extremism is a part of our problem, a symptom of our difficulty, a form of our guilt.

Secondly, our complicity can be found in the profits we make from sex. I know, church people presumably do not hold stock in companies that are peddling pornographic literature. But it is difficult to find a product that is not sold in part through sex appeal. It is extraordinarily difficult to find a movie which does not portray one or another neurotic kind of love relationship. I'm not one who advocates the removal of beautiful girls from advertising nor their abolition from the movies. But neither am I one who finds the conventional forms of business advertising and commercial entertainment altogether healthy in the way they present love and sex. And since we support all this one way or another, we are involved in the perpetration of sickness about sex in our society.

Thirdly, we are involved in complicity by the educational demands of a technological society. We have forcibly postponed the marrying age later and later until teenage marriage is seriously penalized because it has threatened the job possibilities of the male and now of the female. It forces a restraint of sexual attraction and love interest which sometimes goes ten years beyond that which used to be normal in our society, and still is normal in most parts of the world. The normal time when sexual attraction in love would be fully expressed through intercourse is in the mid-teens. It is said that a boy of seventeen is at his lifetime peak of sexuality. This problem of postponed sexual satisfaction is compounded by the self-righteousness of adults who have forgotten their youth or are ashamed of it. It is further compounded by the fact that sexual intercourse is now possible with much less danger of conception than ever before. Many youths are not armed with enough knowledge of conception to avoid it, thus complicating their lives often painfully.

A fourth factor in our complicity is the hypocrisy of marriage. Teenagers see it, sometimes in their own homes, sometimes in the homes of others. You don't have to spend much time with young people to hear them talk of their parents' hollow marriages. The emptiness of many marriages is not lost on the children of those marriages or on their friends. We are part of a culture which has done little to prepare its people for marriage, and one which has allowed millions of marriages to take place which had little chance of success. Such marriages do not illustrate what love and sexuality can mean. Rather they demonstrate the failure of love and the impotence of sexuality.

Finally, we are accomplices because we are part of a civilization which has developed the ability to separate sex from love and sex from procreation. We live in a new era of history as far as sex is concerned. It is an era which most of the world has not yet entered, an era which, indeed, the culture of poverty in our own society has not entered, an era which so far only the upper and middle classes of this country and a few in Europe have entered. It is the era of technological control of conception and venereal disease. Granted, the control is not complete. However, it is still true that we, middle- and upper-class people in the United States and parts of Europe, have come to the point where we can separate love and sex from procreation almost at will.

This means that we have a new responsibility on our hands simply because we have this new possibility.

The situation is that those who have this new power need it least, and those who need it most do not yet have it. The upper and middle classes know how to prevent unwanted children and they have fewer of them anyway. Lower-class people do not know how to prevent unwanted children and they are the ones who have the most. Our responsibility lies in the fact that we have not and often we will not disseminate this knowledge to those who need it most. We keep this knowledge from the lower classes, and from teenagers—the two groups who need it most. This may be right. In any event, we do it. So we are responsible for many avoidable consequences which make sex something to fear. We help turn love in to despair. Really meaningful and useful sex education is virtually non-existent in the country today. Physiology courses in the public school, yes. Moralizing in families and in churches, yes. But only here and there, where someone dares criticism and persists, despite recrimination, are there people introducing either to the lower class or to teenagers the full reality of birth control and what makes for good, lasting love relations. What in the light of this situation is the will of God?

A New Confession

The widely discussed *Confession of 1967* adopted by The United Presbyterian Church, U.S.A., serves as an example of how one denomination, among several, has grasped this issue. The relevant paragraph states:

> The relationship between man and woman exemplifies in a basic way God's ordering of the inter-personal life for which he created mankind. Anarchy in sexual relationships is a symptom of man's alienation from God, his neighbor, and himself. Man's perennial confusion about the meaning of sex has been aggravated in our day by the availability of new means of birth control and the treatment of infection, by the pressures of urbanization, by the exploitation of sexual symbols in mass communication, and by world overpopulation. The church, as the household of God, is called to lead men out of this alienation into the responsible freedom of the new life in Christ.
> Reconciled to God, each person has joy in and respect for his own humanity and that of other persons; a man and a woman are enabled to marry, to commit themselves to a mutually shared life, and to respond to each other in sensitive and lifelong concern; parents receive the grace to care for children in love and to nurture their individuality. The church comes under the judgment of God and invites rejection by man when it fails to lead men and women into the full meaning of life together, or withholds the compassion of Christ from those caught in the moral confusion of our time.
>
> (*The Confession of 1967*, Pt. II, Sec. 4)

Those first two sentences comprise a beautiful theological pair. What they say is that man is incomplete in himself, and sexuality is the most telling form of that incompleteness. Man is made for relatedness. His sexuality is a dramatic form of that relatedness. Man is made for interdependence. Sexuality is a pervasive form of that interdependence.

By implication, this confession is repudiating the Darwinian notion of the nature of man, which makes sex an instrument of conquest. To the contrary, anthropologists, sociologists, and political scientists are now saying that man's first law of survival is mutual aid. This makes sexuality a power for helping one another live. It is when man rejects his need for others, powerfully expressed in his need for a loving partner, that he rejects his true nature and invites his destruction. The way of sexuality, namely, to relate to another, is the way of life, namely, to be interdependent. This is why we read that "the relationship between man and woman exemplifies in a basic way God's ordering of the interpersonal life for which he created mankind." To accept oneself in all of one's sexuality is a fundamental way of accepting oneself as a social being, created to live not in competition with others but in mutual helpfulness and affirmation of others. To reject one's sexuality is one form of rejecting one's interdependence with others. And self-sufficiency carried to its logical extreme means self-destruction. The way a man or a woman handles sexuality is thus a symptom of the way he or she handles the rest of life. Anarchy in sex—refusal to think of anyone but oneself, is symptomatic of the fact that one cannot think of anyone but oneself in all other relationships.

Notice how this statement relates man's sexuality to all the rest of man's relationships. It is a basic form of all relations. There is something welcome, something healthy, something important in this. A biblically based ethic is not repressive when it comes to sex and love. On the contrary, it is expressive. It encourages us to accept as natural and good the power of sexuality. It is a fundamental part of the self, highly symbolic of what one is with others, for better or for worse. Christian faith neither denies that man is sexual or affirms that he is only sexual. It says in effect that only as man seeks positively to integrate the magnificent and terrifying power of sexuality into his whole being can he be himself.

> "Man's perennial confusion about the meaning of sex has been aggravated in our day by the availability of new means for birth control and the treatment of infection, by the pressures of urbanization, by the exploitation of sexual symbols in mass communication, and by world overpopulation."

Here, as in previous sections, following theological reflection on the problem, attention is called to fundamental sociological factors. Here the sociological factors that are mentioned do not include any statement about the decline of morals in our generation. It abstains from invidious comparison between bundling in the eighteenth century and making out in automobiles in the twentieth. The writers of the *Confession* knew that the young people of our generation are more, not less, sensitive to the beauty and wonder of sex and love. In some ways I believe they realized that many young people in our society are more concerned for exercise of responsible and significant love relationships than their elders. That, however, is speculation on my part.

The statement points out the principal factors of contemporary life. It points positively to social factors which confuse and mislead young people as well as the rest of us. First, there is the availability of new means for birth control and the treatment of infection. These advances have fundamentally changed the picture for the sex and love history of mankind, although only a relatively few humans have entered the freedom of this new era as yet.

NEW CONSEQUENCES

This does not mean that there are no consequences in the new era but that there are new consequences. This technological capacity to prevent conception and cure venereal disease does not mean no fears in the future. It means new fears. To put it still another way, this scientific progress with regard to control of conception and disease does not mean there will be no sanctions. It means there will have to be new sanctions. Why?

Because it makes possible new forms of exploiting people, new betrayals, betrayals of trust, new disappointments in love. There is nothing worse than being dehumanized, used as a thing rather than communed with as a person. Birth control won't help us avoid that. You can cure all the VD in the world and not prevent one case of the misuse of people. Indeed, the new freedom given us by technology in the area of sex and love only opens up an era of greater exploitation unless we learn what it means to love rightly and make sex the expression of that love. What I'm saying is, the new technology won't reduce the figures on broken hearts. It could increase them. No fear any more? Nonsense. The fear of being tricked, the fear of being misused, the fear of being rejected; these fears will now become more real as the old fears of pregnancy and disease disappear. New sanctions, therefore, will be needed, new ideals of what love is, new sensitivities as to the beauty and the ugliness of sexual relations. Let's face it, a sexual relation can either be a communion or a catastrophe. It can either mean an ultimate expression of love and respect or be the final refuge of empty people. Birth control and VD cures aren't going to determine the quality of love relations. The era of greatest challenge in matters of sex and love is ahead of us. We face the prospect of the ultimate hollowness of sexual activity. We face also the possibility that it can express a wonderful wholeness of respect and affection. Because man is man he wants meaningful relations with sex, not meaningless relations. He wants wholeness not hollowness. New sanctions will develop, therefore. They will not be sanctions based on fears of pregnancy and venereal disease. They will be sanctions based on a positive ideal of love, and the way sex is used to express love. Don't forget this, above all: technology hasn't changed the fact that every sex act has *meaning*. As long as the sex act has meaning it means something wonderful or something horrible. That's why we'll always need a sense of values with regard to sexual expression. The new thing is: these values will have to be positive ideals, not, as they have too often been, negative inhibitions.

POPULATION PRESSURES

Pressures of urbanization are another of the factors we will have to deal with. Most people are now living in metropolitan areas with all the freedom and the anonymity that this provides. With the chance this brings for experimentation in sex and love, urbanization offers a promise and threat. The promise is one of establishing relationships no longer because we have to establish them, as we did in the small towns because we had to. We were expected to be friendly with everybody whether we liked them or not. The new basis of friendship is that you decide who you will cultivate as a friend—urban life gives new freedom to do this. The threat of urbanization, however, is that you may not be able to establish any close ties. They aren't ready-made, as they were in the small towns of yesteryear. What this means for sex and love is a new era of permissiveness and of strangeness: permission to enter into new experiences but little support from the community, and therefore, perhaps little success in making friends, let alone falling in love.

The Confession of 1967 speaks of the exploitation of sexual symbols in mass communication as contributing to confusion about sexuality. Sex is big business today. Sex means money in the mass media of advertising and entertainment. This use of sex to sell anything from soap to motor oil can't help but distort the meaning of sexuality, and give it what Erich Fromm calls a "marketing orientation." This culture makes it hard not to think of sexuality (one's own or another's) as something to be "sold" instead of thinking of sexuality as something to be given, or withheld, in affection and respect.

World population, says *Confession of 1967*, also contributes to our confusion about the meaning of sexuality. How so? The world population is growing at the rate of two per cent per year. Between 1850 and 1950 it doubled—one hundred years. United Nations experts say it will double again between now and the year 2010— forty years. By that time there will be a world population of six billion people. How has this problem—devastating as it is—served to confuse man about sexuality? Strictly answered, the need to limit sexual activity is growing more and more necessary as far as procreation is concerned, therefore, there is an increasing tolerance for the use of birth control. Whereas, in conservative Christian circles of the past, it was regarded as a sin to do anything to avoid conception, this is increasingly thought to be meritorious. The population problem has become so serious for Japan that it has legalized abortion. Any woman can request it of the doctors. The trend is clearly stated by Joseph Fletcher: "Sex is indeed for recreation as well as procreation and the over-population of the world will emphasize re-creation more and more." The idea of separating sexual activity from conception while using it for communion will be more and more acceptable. The time is not far off when nations will limit the production of children by law, and sex will be limited almost entirely to communion. This is inevitably creating a climate for sexual expression outside of marriage.

The Confession of 1967 goes on. It says that the church is called "to lead men out of this alienation into the responsible freedom of the new life in Christ." The key to Christian ethics is responsible freedom. There is more freedom to handle sexuality differently than before. There is more right use of this freedom. The Christian is responsible to Christ for the way he uses his freedom. It is freedom from law and freedom for love. This means a great deal. It means that no laws, customs, or honored practices are the final determinants of conduct for the Christian. Christ is the only Lord and love is the only law for the Christian. But, by the same token, love means unconditional responsibility—no neat limits, such as law allows. Law says, "You are responsible this much and no more." Love says, "You are responsible all the way, without end."

There are at least two parts to a love ethic: it involves a motive and it involves a concern for consequences.

The motive of that responsible freedom in Christ which the church is bound to seek in its own life and proclaim to the world —the motive is thanksgiving: thanksgiving for what God has done for us in Christ. Luther called it a eucharistic ethic: thanksgiving to God for what he has done for us, and therefore a desire to express that love in whatever we do to whomever we do it. This is one way of saying what sexuality is. It is something to be thankful for. It is a gift of God. We are to use it as a gift of God. If sex relations are what they ought be for Christians they will be nothing less than celebration.

MARRIAGE

Some years ago a progressive statement on marriage was published by the Vatican. *The New Yorker* magazine commented favorably upon the Pope's statement. It was a far-reaching document because it stated not only the conventional idea that marriage is for the purpose of procreation but the new idea that it is for communion, too. But, said *The New Yorker,* the Pope missed one thing about marriage that he really could not have been expected to understand. Nowhere did he say anything about the fact that marriage is fun! Sexuality, rightly experienced, is fun—more, it is joy—celebration.

A second part of the Christian love ethic is concern for consequences, both immediate and long range. It is imperative to ask what a particular use expression of sexuality will do: to me (self-love) and to the other (other-love). Self-love and other-love ought never to be separated. They are two forms of the basic capacity to affirm life. If one cannot understand one's self, one cannot understand others. If one cannot accept one's self, one cannot accept others. If one cannot discipline one's self, one cannot discipline others. If one cannot forgive one's self, one cannot forgive others. The concern for the immediate and the long-range consequences of what a sexual relation does to me and what it does to the other is a vital part of the Christian ethic. We should be teaching our children to ask questions about consequences, and we should always ask these questions of ourselves.

The Confession of 1967 then says,

> "Reconciled to God, each person has joy in and respect for his own humanity and that of other persons."

This is the only section of any confession I know which deals explicitly with pre-marital relations. It deals with other relations, too, to be sure, but as you will see in a moment, the next two sections of this one sentence deals sequentially with marital relations and with parenthood.

What does it say? It says, "each person has joy in and respect for his own humanity and that of other persons." I mentioned that Christian love is motivated by thanksgiving and has a concern for consequences. Taken together, these represent what is called here "joy in and respect for one's own humanity and that of other persons." This does not give us rules with regard to pre-marital intercourse, petting, necking or, to cover all of them, making out. What is most important for us, as well as for teenagers, is that we learn what it means to respect, to love, to affirm, to exercise long-range good-will toward ourselves and one another.

This means that where teenagers are not instructed by their parents or medically supervised in the use of contraceptives they should not engage in premarital intercourse. Without proper instruction, without medical supervision, neither the pill nor any other means of birth control can be confidently counted on to avoid that disastrous consequence: the unwanted child.

In other words, there are practical implications of this stress on respect for oneself and others. But we have to draw out these implications. Here we should remember that the unwanted child can still be somebody and the forced marriage can still amount to something. Our attitude toward the consequences of irresponsible love must be responsible, which means redemptive.

The Confession goes on to speak of marital relations:

> "A man and a woman are enabled to marry, to commit themselves to a mutually shared life, and to respond to each other in sensitive and life-long concern."

Here marriage is emphasized as a gift. It is a power some have—not necessarily given to all. *Confession 67* emphasizes marriage as a commitment to share life and possessions to the end. The great stress here is on marriage as a form of Christian community, expressive of what all life ought to be: mutually shared.

PARENTHOOD

This *Confession* has an unusual way of talking about parenthood: "Parents receive the grace to care for children in love and nurture their individuality."

Nothing is said here about discipline, in spite of all the efforts to stress a return to punishment of children for wrong-doing. *Confession 67*'s concern is with the human potential of children. This ought to be the principle concern of the parent, it implies. The personhood of the child is underlined by the word individuality. Parents receive the grace, says the *Confession*, "to care for children in love and to nurture their individuality." This is a unique emphasis for any confession. Normally, when you get to children in an official church document you get counsel which sounds like father knows best—highly paternalistic. You hear words about children obeying their parents. As a father I strongly approve. I insist on it with my children (without saying whether or not I get it!). But *Confession '67* talks about caring and about nurturing individuality.

Now to the anathema. This statement comes as close as a confession could possibly come in the modern era to warning about the hell that will follow if you don't believe:

> "The church comes under the judgment of God and invites rejection by man when it fails to lead men and women into the full meaning of life together, or withholds the compassion of Christ from those caught in the moral confusion of our time."

In other words, there are two things which will separate us from God and doom the church, as far as the world is concerned. One of them is failure to convey by word and work a positive understanding of sex and a convincing interpretation of married life. The age of the taboo is gone. The time for negatives is over. The place for prohibition is past. Not that these things have no more importance. It's just that none of these things or all of them together is enough. The church has a far larger, more difficult, and beautiful task. That is, to lead men and women and boys and girls into an understanding of the mystery and the goodness of sexuality, the wonder and the possibilities of human relations patiently cultivated and loyally continued. Only in the context of positive preaching and practice will the church avoid the judgment of God and the ridicule of the world.

The other thing we are soberly warned about is this. We'd better be positive about the way we treat those who have made mistakes in sex and love. Our job is to be redemptive rather than repressive. Those who have made mistakes are often suffering untold problems as a result. They are receiving their judgment already. Those who have misused sexual powers, abused freedom, misunderstood what personal relationships ought to be, ought not to be dealt with finally in discipline, finally in judgment, finally in punishment. Not that these things are ruled out, but that none of them individually or all of them together are enough. Discipline is for the purpose of guidance. Judgment has in it a warning. Punishment is for the sake of reform. The Christian task is to help the person learn from what he has experienced. First of all, this is done by relating to him as one sinner to another, since that is what we are, too. Censorship, isolation, imprisonment can never be a final action of Christian people. None of these approaches, however necessary to put a curb on extreme behavior, will be enough for us. We will seek by every means at our disposal to treat those who have mistaken their goals, misused their freedom, and misunderstood what it means to be human—we will extend our efforts to find ways to help them back into the community of faith, the church, and back into the community of law, the state.

10

A Humanistic View of
Sexual Relationship

•

LESTER A. KIRKENDALL

Convinced that the institutional church has serious difficulties both in dealing with moral issues and with unorthodox individuals like himself, Dr. Kirkendall brings to this symposium a valuable critical stance from his vantage point as scholar and humanist. A professor of family life at Oregon State University, he has written several books, the best known being *Premarital Intercourse and Interpersonal Relations*. He is also co-editor of *Sex in The Adolescent Years: New Directions In Guiding and Teaching Youth*.

•

FOR THE HUMANIST the concern and justification for morality arises from the need to help man live in an increasingly complex world, and at the same time to experience himself as a fulfilled, responsible, social human being. Moral practices should help man develop his humane capacities to the maximum and create circumstances which will support ever-widening circles of social interaction. The humanist feels that there is no supernatural for man to look to for help or intervention. Man has made his problems; if solutions are to come they must come from him. He is the architect of both his triumphs and his failures.

The humanist sees authority as being derived from a knowledge of the nature of man, for it is man who is to be served through morality. To this end one must know as much as possible about man and his needs, and about the consequences and effects of various procedures which may be used in meeting these needs. He supports the authority of knowledge derived from processes of rational, systematic inquiry, and asks how this knowledge can be related to the important objective.

A good example of the problems facing those who hold that authority is derived from divine revelation is found in the uproar in the Catholic Church over the encyclical, *Humanae Vitae*, which bans the use of the birth control pill. Actually, barring use of the pill is a secondary issue. The primary issue is whether Papal dictum, representing an imposed theistic authority, is an acceptable approach to ordering the sexual and reproductive behavior of human beings. The protest which has resulted indicates that many Catholics think not. Cardinal O'Boyle of Washington, D.C., was correct when he said the protests of the Catholic priests in his diocese broke down the authority of the church. In other words, Cardinal O'Boyle was facing a rebellion, and he knew it. Imposed pronouncements which rest upon supernaturalistic authority are less able to motivate behavior now. The theological concept which the Pope used to support his dictum was based upon ideas concerning the "natural" use of sex. Traditionally, Catholic theologians have taught that in the performance of the sex act no barrier to procreative outcomes is acceptable; potential reproductive outcomes must in no way be circumvented. But now even devout Catholics are asking by what right and through what logic Catholic teachings presume to limit the natural use of sex so narrowly.

The humanist, facing the question of the proper use of sex, would ask what effect various alternatives would have upon helping human beings realize their personal and social potentialities. What would make them more loving, more vibrant beings, and at the same time more responsible and appreciative of others and their needs? He would ask what empirical evidence is available to help answer these questions. He would depend heavily upon rational processes, though recognizing that emotions, too, are involved.

Some of the same questions, of course, would be asked by Christians. This must be acknowledged. But it must also be acknowledged that seeking answers from empirical evidence forecloses the possibility of tidy black-white answers which come from citing "God's will." Those Christians who have moved away from this simplistic approach can testify that as a result problem solving becomes more complex and uncertain. That is the way life is.

SEX ACTS AND PERSONS

Religious concern with sex, as is the case with our whole culture, has concentrated on sex acts and the number of persons involved in them. Has masturbation or homosexuality occurred, and how many have expressed themselves sexually in this manner? How many have been involved in extramarital relationships? These are the terms in which we have typically painted a picture of contemporary sexual behavior. This preoccupation with the omission or commission of acts, reflected and reinforced by the organized church, keeps us at the taxonomic level. Sexual behavior is discussed in terms of specific acts and the frequency with which they occur.

In order to understand the humanistic meaning of sexuality, discussion must be in terms of the quality and processes of sexual relationships. What do they mean to the persons involved and, beyond them, to the whole society? I attempted to spell out this approach in my research on premarital intercourse. In this study, reported in *Premarital Intercourse and Interpersonal Relationships*, I sought to determine whether premarital sexual experience contributed to or detracted from the capacity of individuals to relate responsibly and loyally to one another and to others. To arrive at an answer I found it necessary to look at other processes and interaction rather than at incidence figures. I was concerned with the quality of commmunication, degree of affectional involvement, probable motivations, maturational levels, readiness and capacity for assuming responsibility, and evidences of maturity or immaturity.

When the phenomenon of premarital intercourse was so regarded, it no longer appeared to be simply episodic with each experience like every other. Ordinarily we talk as though intercourse with a prostitute had the same meaning as intercourse with a fiancée. Using the factors I enumerated as criteria for evaluating the sexual relationship made it very clear that as human relations experiences (and, yes, as sexual experiences) these two levels of intercourse are very different.

Some statistical data were collected and reported, in order to ascertain trends and learn something of the extent of the practice. But the report on the data comprised only 44 pages of the 304 pages of the book, and this part was used as an appendix. The remainder of the book was devoted to a discussion of the qualitative rather than the quantitative aspects of premarital intercourse.

I have noted that in our culture we give a disproportionate amount of attention to premarital intercourse, and knowledge that individuals have either accepted or rejected this experience has been used to determine the quality of their morals. An unmarried person who engaged in premarital sexual relations was, *ipso facto*, "immoral," "promiscuous" or "sinful." The question of the degree of responsibility, affection, or loyalty which entered into the relationship was given no consideration. ‣

At times I am asked whether the younger generation is more or less moral than their parents or grandparents. My questioners always expect an answer in terms of incidence figures. If I could prove that a larger percentage of one generation than of another engaged in premarital intercourse, then we would know which generation was the less moral. The questioners do not expect a discussion about differences in attitudes, the processes of relating, or the philosophy which underlies decision making.

But now I must face my own challenge. How can the humanist paint a picture of contemporary sexual behavior without dwelling on incidence figures? Can he go beyond the act-centered focus? What does he talk about? The following seem to me to be features which are important enough to receive consideration in a discussion of contemporary sexual behavior.

1. *Punitive attitudes toward those deviating from conventional standards are declining.* A rapidly increasing acceptance of contraceptives, a greater willingness to give rehabilitative help to premaritally pregnant girls, growing strength of effort to liberalize legal restrictions on abortions and homosexuality, less condemnation of premarital intercourse, talk of establishing marital visiting arrangements for persons in prison, and a general acceptance of masturbation as a legitimate, normal practice are all evidences of this trend. The attitudes of the general public on matters such as these seem to be more liberal than the attitudes of those responsible for institutional practices and policies. For example, Catholic lay people have consistently been more ready than the church authorities to accept contraceptive practices. The number of Catholic couples patronizing family planning clinics in various communities is often as large proportionately as the number of non-Catholics.

The decline of punitiveness inevitably raises the question as to what is happening to morals. Are they declining? The big debate, as might be expected, has been over premarital intercourse. How seriously, if at all, have permissive attitudes corrupted youth? The answer to this is not clear. We are not sure whether there is more premarital intercourse than formerly. Neither are we sure what degree of responsibility or irresponsibility is associated with the premarital intercourse which does occur. May it be, if we define morality in humanistic rather than in legalistic terms, that young people are becoming more moral?

This could certainly be, for some of the young people who accept and participate in premarital intercourse espouse a standard which has integrity and which is more humane than that exemplified by their pious critics. For while these adults are demanding simply abstention from an act, the young people are going beyond acts to argue that all behavior needs to be viewed in light of the human need for love and respect. They are sincerely concerned with erasing the hoary double standard. This should be good news to everyone, especially religious leaders.

Many modern youth are deeply concerned for human beings, and they see the furtherance of human welfare as basic to all behavior. Thus they arrive at a criterion for decision-making which they apply to all behavior. With full consistency they oppose legalistic sex standards at the same time they disapprove our military involvement in Vietnam.

Recently after I had given the opening address at a symposium on "Sexuality and Human Relationships," a small group of youth who had been in the audience stopped me for a two-hour conversation. They were engaged in picketing and demonstrating against the involvement of their university in Defense Department contracts, and wished to discuss their feelings, attitudes and experiences. In the whole conversation sex was never mentioned. I couldn't help thinking how much more comfortable it would be for some people if this group could return to the traditional absorption of youth in sex!

These youth see the various issues as expressions of rigidity, as struggles for power, or expressions of egocentricity which violate the principle of deep concern for the needs and welfare of others.

Can the church itself meet this level of morality? When one notes the extent to which sexual behavior is made a more serious offense than discriminatory practices or physical and psychological violence, and the complacency, even acceptance, by the church of various of our social, economic, and political practices, the answer must be no. There is more hope for the future in this group of humanistically-oriented youth than in those who adhere rigidly to traditional religious practices.

For those who are preoccupied with conventional patterns of sexual behavior it is worth noting that, when youth apply these humanistic patterns, they are often surprisingly conservative. In their behavior many of them are as conservative as their critics. The difference lies in the reasons for their behavior. Ira Reiss, who conducted extensive studies on sexual standards and permissiveness, points out that according to his studies, "the vast majority" of teenagers are "quite conservative and restrained" in the area of premarital sex behavior.

The religious moralist loses sight of the broader picture of sexual morality when he brings his authority to bear so inflexibly upon the act of premarital intercourse and its prevention. Every counselor has met people who are ridden with guilt or living dysfunctionally, sexually and otherwise, because of the heavy repressions to which they were subjected in early life. All too often these persons are transmitting their frustrations and difficulties to others —children, spouses, friends. A pattern of rigid conformity can be imposed upon at least some individuals, but at a crippling cost psychologically speaking. One is forced to ask what price is worth paying for our conventional sex standards. Are two or three years of additional virginity worth the cost which is exacted in attaining them?

2. *A growing willingness for males to accept their share of the responsibility in sexual participation is observable.* This development is not very advanced, but its beginning can be documented. I have talked with unmarried males who have gone with their female partners to family planning clinics to learn about contraceptive practices, and to the personnel of family planning clinics who

have talked with such couples. Males have talked with me about the substitution of petting to climax for intercourse as a means of protecting the couple from pregnancy. Others have expressed a real distaste for intercourse which is engaged in as a furtive, non-affectional, advantage-taking experience. Others have come to realize the inherent unfairness of the double standard and have moved to discard it. All of this means that the moral emphasis is being moved from the sex act itself to a concern for eliminating exploitive behavior, and for seeing that unwanted pregnancies and unwanted children are not produced. Does this represent responsible sex behavior?

Self-governorship and non-exploitive behavior such as unmarried youth can display toward one another in the realm of sex come far more from experiencing love and support from the important persons in their lives than they do from the imposition of standards. Persons who, in their family, school and community interactions, have found joy and satisfaction in the exercise of their various personal and social capacities, are able to deal responsibly with their impulses, appetites and desires. I learned long ago that when I find an individual who is in trouble with his sexuality—who is demeaning himself and exploiting others—he is almost certain to be one who has little respect for himself. His sense of self-worth is low and his self-image damaged. Conversely, an individual able to deal with his sexuality in non-exploitive ways, who can feel that his sexuality is an enriching capacity rather than an over-powering drive—such an individual is very likely to be one who has a sense of achievement and worth. Having received love and respect from others, he can give these in return; his self-image is a positive one. Such persons are by no means always virgins; some enjoy active and responsible sexual associations. But they are not pushed into these relationships by neurotic, compulsive needs. They are able to accept these experiences, live with them, or terminate them responsibly as they do other relationship experiences.

3. *A clear rejection by many youth of hypocrisy and dishonesty in our sexual practices can be noted.* I have met couples who, having decided to enter upon intercourse, have told their families that

such was their intention. They did not wish to profess one thing and live another. The rejection of aspects of the double standard is largely due to the recognition of its inherent dishonesty and hypocrisy. Protests against the hypocritical positions into which our "preach this, but do that" approach to sex forces us is common in youth groups. *Playboy*, I am convinced, gained much of its popularity and influence because of its exposure of such contradictions.

4. *An acceptance of the right of an individual to the fullest possible enjoyment of his various capacities within socially responsible limits is being extended to sex.* While there is a strand of hedonism in this development, it is certainly not wholly hedonistic. And even if it is, some will ask, why not, so long as exploitation and misuse of others is not involved. Beyond this is the growing acceptance of the view that the exercise of a human capacity is desirable if the capacity is to be retained and integrated into the total personality. This view leads professionals interested in the possibility of a full life for older people to be concerned with the continuation of sexual activity into old age. Likewise it raises questions concerning the consequences of the sexual inhibitions which are urged upon children and youth. Do they to some degree lose their capacity for responsiveness? The supposition that this may be true leads the Roys in *Honest Sex* to suggest that many religious leaders might be more human and less self-righteous if they experienced more frequent erotic arousal.

5. *Respect for institutional structures simply because they are institutional structures is clearly lessening.* The following illustration shows how we rigidify institutional structure. A conference of marriage counselors which I attended was devoted to exploring the significance of extramarital sexual relationships. Various conferees presented case histories involving infidelity. As they did so I became aware that in each history the person outside the marriage who was sexually involved with the spouse was referred to as "the third party." This person was never described in any detail, nor did any of the counselors seem much concerned with what the "third party" was like. The feeling gradually developed that the

"third party" was a shadowy interloper who could settle the whole matter immediately were he obliging enough to go off somewhere and drop dead. As I reflected I realized that in my undergraduate marriage classes, composed largely of unmarried students, I too had dealt with triangles. Under these circumstances, however, there had been no third party. I was simply dealing with three human beings who were in a jam and needed help. But let two of them go through the wedding ceremony, and I had, *ipso facto*, a "third party," with all the sinister connotations attached thereto.

Similar observations could be made about the rigid attitudes toward divorce. A marked evolution in thinking about divorce will be necessary before traditional Christians can ask, as the Roys do in their book:

> How easy should divorce be made? Should there be marriage-divorce counselors who sometimes would actually advocate divorce and make the transition easier? Ultimately, is not a divorce a matter of consent, and if a couple simply decides—without the typically required rift and accompanying agony—to terminate a marriage, is that a less Christian decision than to struggle through years of gradual decay? . . .
>
> The Church may become free to equate divorce not with sin but with a major change of business or professional work after a failure.

The possibility of outcomes which might result from a more humanistic approach to divorce was clarified for me by a fifteen-year-old boy who was doing yard work for us. He came to say that he would not be able to work for a week, maybe not for two weeks. His mother and sister and he were going to California. I inquired if the objective was sightseeing. "No," he told me, "we're going down to visit my father and his wife. We do this each summer. They either come to Oregon to visit us, or we go to California to visit them. Two years ago we had such a good time that we stayed for two weeks instead of the one we had originally planned."

I wish that these breaks in intimate relationships did not have to occur. But I hope I am concerned sincerely enough with human beings to ask and study such questions as these: How can we help people into relationships which have enough strength so that disrupting breaks can be avoided? If breaks must come, how can the best interest of all be served? How can those who have been parties to a relationship be helped to part, not as mortal enemies, but as friends?

The frequency with which unmarried couples set up arrangements for living together without going through the marriage ceremony is another example of movement away from a rigid institutional structure. Still another is the growing willingness on the part of adoption agencies to permit single persons to adopt and rear a child.

6. *Our society is characterized by a growing depersonalization which has its impact upon sexual expression.* This complicates the search for meaningful, responsible sexual expression. Many persons, deprived of warm, loving associations in their families and in the surroundings in which they mature, seek in casual, irresponsible sexual associations, the satisfactions they have missed elsewhere. Having been emotionally damaged, they are impelled to exploit others. They are searching for the closeness and intimacy which they have missed elsewhere. The conduct of these people is often referred to as "promiscuous behavior." A much more accurate description would be to refer to it as "deprivation" or "starvation" behavior. In a highly depersonalized society, more and more devoid of close human contacts, as ours is seemingly becoming, references to casual sexual relationships as "intimate behavior" become increasingly inappropriate. What is probably happening is that more and more people are having contacts which involve physical closeness without intimacy.

7. *With the development of more openness and a more relaxed attitude toward sexuality has come a more sharply defined and organized opposition to these trends.* This is especially true as it relates to any institutional recognition of these developments and any changes to accommodate to them. Sex education in the schools is an especially clear example of the crystallization of opposition. The same holds true also for any attempt to lighten legal restrictions, as for example, those having to do with such matters as abortion, homosexuality, and penalties for the sale of pornography.

8. *Distortions of the meaning and character of human sexuality through the mass media have continued, probably even increased.* The tie between sex and the competitive emphasis inherent in the profit motive is clear. The extent to which human sexuality can be conditioned by still other aspects of the social structure is quite evident. The need is to set sexual expression firmly in the context of the processes of responsible human relating, and there is evidence that this is the direction in which we are moving.

9. *Inflexibility in traditional concepts concerning sex and sex roles makes realistic attitudes and understanding extremely hard to come by.* Attitude changes come very slowly. Research may demonstrate the inaccuracy of certain points of view toward sex, or clinical evidence may clearly show particular concepts to be erroneous. Yet the error persists, perhaps not in its most blatant form, but it persists.

Masturbation is a case in point. Writers and speakers now commonly accept the view that masturbation in itself is a harmless practice, yet they very often conclude a discussion with some comment which shows their incapacity to assimilate the point of view they have just presented. For example, I recently came across a writer who presented the modern liberal, accepting view of adolescent masturbation. But he closed his statement by asserting that adolescents must be made to understand that masturbation was not "acceptable public behavior," and had to be controlled. When one thinks of the extent to which adolescents *do not* practice masturbation in public, what is the need of this injunction? The only conclusion I can reach is that it represents a clinging to outmoded strictures about masturbation which the writer simply could not abandon completely. He could not rest until he had expressed at least token allegiance to the old concepts.

These traditional concepts are most effective blinders. For example Scandinavian sexual attitudes and practices, especially those of Sweden, have always mystified Americans and have been widely misunderstood. This, I suspect, is because Scandinavian attitudes and practices are much more within the humanistic framework than are the traditional Christian ones. The American looking at

Sweden has typically seen only the more relaxed and accepting Swedish attitude toward premarital intercourse. More than one American critic has regarded this as the central issue in the Swedish attitude toward sex.

The Swedes do not see it this way, however. Their central concern is with providing a situation and working out a philosophy which will enable men and women to share equally and responsibly as human beings in their family, business and social experiences. An interesting and informative book which exemplifies this view is *Sex and Society in Sweden* by Brigitta Linner. She deals principally with the development of sex roles, discussing the way in which such experiences as premarital intercourse, extramarital intercourse, divorce, and parental responsibilities affect men and women. She discusses such matters as economic remuneration in the world of work and educational patterns in relation to sex roles. Two illustrations will indicate the character and scope of her approach. She suggests, in terms of a basic concern for equal privileges and equal responsibilities for men and women, that in case of divorce the wife rather than the husband might be required to pay alimony. Or when both husband and wife work, the family might decide to change residence to provide the wife an improved economic and occupational situation.

Yet Mrs. Linner's book, and Swedish attitudes toward sex in general, have been criticized as being focused mainly on premarital intercourse. A more humanistic and less limited view would enable Americans to see more clearly what is actually being said and sought in Sweden.

10. *Certain rifts and cleavages make it clear that meaningful dialogue on sexual matters as it involves particular segments of the population is agonizingly difficult, if not impossible.* I have in mind, on the one hand, the open, intelligent, questioning and, on the whole, altruistic student leaders of our colleges and universities, and, on the other, those persons who are usually, but by no means always, fifty years of age or older, and who are by their own designation, Christians. These two groups, mainly due to the in-

transigence and rigidities of those in the older group, find it virtually impossible to communicate.

The drama and the final impasse which often results from such
an effort was classically played out in a three-day symposium held
at Oklahoma State University in November, 1968. Several of the
student organizations financed and sponsored "Sexpo '68," a three-
day symposium on various aspects of human sexuality, to which
they invited as speakers a number of local religious and medical
leaders and three outside speakers, Dr. Albert Ellis of New York
City, Dr. Edward Hobbs of the Pacific School of Religion, and
me. The views of the outside speakers anticipated and recommended changes but their views were not new to anyone who had
followed their utterances and writings. The initial speeches and
the ensuing discussions were candid and forthright, and student
response was excellent. Time and time again rooms were filled to
overflowing by students who came to hear and participate in discussions on abortion, birth control, marriage, homosexuality, premarital sex, premarital standards, and sex education. The students'
questions were penetrating, their elation with the experience of
open interchange was obvious. The enthusiastic exchanges in the
plenary session were carried immediately to the halls of the Student Union, the dinner tables of the living organizations, and the
informal talk fests of fraternities and sororities. I personally heard
many students remark on their pleasure and satisfaction with the
chance to talk with each other and the speakers on these topics.
"We've never had anything like this before." "I've never before
been able to talk about such matters with anyone." "Talking about
these subjects openly makes dealing with them intelligently so
much easier."

The students clearly were thinking critically; they were weighing
and evaluating, accepting and rejecting. No one could have swal-
lowed every view presented and escaped massive ideological indi-
gestion; the views were so dissimilar that critical evaluation had to
take place.

But simultaneously with the growing enthusiasm of the students, a solid rock of non-comprehension and fear appeared. It was

on this rock that genuine communication foundered. The fear was expressed that "the young people were being influenced." Various persons in the audiences began asking how these views could be reconciled with "religion" and/or "Christianity." Did the speakers believe "the Bible was the inspired Word of God"? "Sir, are you a Christian?" "What's wrong with being a Christian?"

Intransigence and dogmatic stances became increasingly visible and were only intensified when a similarly dogmatic attitude was manifested by any of the speakers—for it must be acknowledged that dogmatic attitudes play no favorites. The real issue, it became increasingly clear, was whether anyone with long and deep emotional investment in a particular ideology was able to think objectively or to be flexible. At the same time the early student enthusiasm for openness and communication seemed dampened, and the rightist position hardened.

The result was that a few hours before the closing of the symposium the President of the University gave out a press release which said:

"In no way are the recent expressions regarding sex as presented by certain off-campus speakers on the OSU campus representative of the positions of the Oklahoma State University.

"Although willing to hear other points of view, the University's position in matters of sex and sex education continues in the Judaeo-Christian tradition, a position which also has been presented by various speakers from both on and off campus in recent days."

This was probably because those who held the traditional position were either in the power positions of the University structure, or had access to channels of communication which led to those in power. A source close to the President said he had received "a lot of calls" expressing negative reactions to the Sexpo program.

This recital would be pointless except for the fact that it occurs too often to be exceptional. Over and over I have seen adults dismally muff their opporunities to communicate with youth. Such experiences are disheartening and disillusioning. In the sexual area and in others, I have seen student groups attempt to open honest and forthright interchange with adults only to experience rebuffs similar to the one just described. And all too often the squelch is administered in the name of "Christian love."

One of the reasons for such an outcome are those blinders, discussed in point #9, imposed by traditional concepts toward premarital intercourse. It is extremely difficult for the older traditionally oriented religious person to understand how feelings have changed since his own youth. For this person to try to talk with today's youth in the framework within which he thought and acted is almost certain to mean no communication. The generation of youth growing up in the 1910's, 1920's and even in the 1930's was a generation imbued with the double standard philosophy. The male was supposed to push for "all he could get," the girl was to "draw the line." If she "gave in" then she was supposed to be overwhelmed with guilt, and the male "lost respect" for her. And over each hung the depressing knowledge that he had transgressed—he had violated a sacred rule. The fear of pregnancy and severe community disapproval were other factors which wielded a profoundly retarding influence.

Today, however, fears have been largely dispelled, the feeling of transgression has been displaced by the concept that this is a matter to be decided upon in the light of circumstances, and there is much more awareness of mutual responsibility. Not all youth have developed these concepts, of course, but enough have that those adults who try to communicate with youth in terms of the feelings and assumptions of a generation or two ago are likely to find the going very difficult.

Current discussions about "morality" (a term which I hope we can soon drop in favor of terms which will describe mature, responsible human behavior) usually focus, as has been noted, upon a supposed increase in non-marital sexual activity. Those who make immorality and participation in sex acts synonymous usually see current developments as threatening and evil. On the other hand, looking at sex from a humanistic point of view, one may be encouraged by a greater openness, what seems to be an increasing concern with responsible relating, a concern for associating sex

with affection, and a perspective which is calling for a reassessment and re-evaluation of the place of sex in life. This cannot be
demonstrated statistically, but these are the hopeful developments
which one must chronicle as he "paints a picture of contemporary
sexual behavior." This has also to be the humanist's way of talking
about sex. I look forward to the day when discussions of "morality"
will be displaced by discussions about what we can do to help man
attain his full stature as a human being, how he can become more
responsible, more sensitive to himself and others, more genuine,
more honest, more trusting and trustworthy—in short how he can
become an alert, vibrant, loving, fulfilled human being. If this kind
of person is not what should come from our moral strivings then I
want nothing to do with morality.

11

Responsibility for Life:
Sex as Communion

•

CYNTHIA C. WEDEL

Believing that the startling sexual freedom of our day may actually lead to placing the physical aspects of marriage in better perspective, Dr. Wedel argues for deep interpersonal communion between man and woman. The associate general secretary of the National Council of Churches of Christ, U.S.A., she is the author of *Employed Women And The Church* and co-author with Janet Tulloch of *Happy Issue*. She also contributed a chapter to the previous symposium in this series, *Sex, Family and Society In Theological Focus*.

WHAT IS THE PLACE of marriage and the family in God's plan for his human children? This is a presumptuous question, for none of us can pretend to comprehend the wisdom or the plan of God. But surely it is our business, as reasonably intelligent Christians, to try to think theologically about our lives, and to share these thoughts openly with one another for mutual correction and amendment.

I always marvel at the chance God took in creating a creature "like unto himself—in his own image." He certainly didn't have to do it! The universe could be a wonderful place without us, and if God were creating it for his own pleasure, one imagines that he could have enjoyed it for endless aeons as the seasons and planets and animals and vegetation developed and changed and followed the intricate laws he had devised for them.

Yet he created man—the one creature to whom he gave freedom. Freedom to make choices, freedom to say yes or no, freedom even to turn against his creator. And God, in his infinite wisdom, must have known that such a creature would exercise his freedom, would say no, would make tragically wrong choices. Yet freedom is not real unless it includes all these possibilities—as every parent knows.

Why should God have done this? I can find only one reason. It was because he wanted to create love. (I'm not sure how to say this—if God is love, perhaps it is wrong to say he created it—perhaps it would be more accurate to say that he wanted to share his own quality of love with his creation.) And he knew that love, in the highest sense, must always be a completely free and uncoerced gift. In a sense, each of the parties in a love relationship must be able to say no—to refuse the relationship. Only then can it be real. God no doubt loves all of his creation; and quite possibly other things and creatures respond to his love. But as far as we can tell their responses are instinctual, unconscious. A creature with whom he could have a relationship of mutual love had to be free.

So God took the chance and created man and woman—capable of loving or not loving one another and himself. And, being human, they exercised their freedom, disobeyed their creator, and suffered the consequences. Yet God never stopped loving. All the remainder of the Bible, and indeed all of human history, can be read as a story of God's unceasing attempts to win his human creatures to respond to his love in loving obedience to him. And shining through the pages of history, we see the points of bright light when some man or woman has responded fully to God's love —these are the ones we call the saints. Most of them were painfully ordinary people—but by the simple act of completely open response to God they, and sometimes the age in which they lived, were transformed.

Once, we Christians believe, God himself came into human life in the form of his son to give us, in terms that we could grasp and comprehend, what he really meant human life to be like. But with our human skill in rejecting God, we crucified him, and have, more often than not, twisted our interpretation of his life and his words to suit our own convenience.

But what all of this says to me is that God has a hope, a dream, a plan for what human life can and should be. Looking at Jesus Christ we see a man in whom the self-centeredness and self-protectiveness which poisons most human life seemed to be entirely missing. He was truly "a man for others"—so open and caring and loving that his mere presence was a healing. His life exhibits no morbid fear, no anxiety, and a wonderful sense of proportion of what was important and unimportant.

I could analyze further our Lord's remarkable example to us of what human life might be. But the point of all this is to suggest that God does, indeed, have something in mind for us. Life could be whole, and free, and creative and joyous, and human beings could be loving, and unafraid and happy. And the family is the place where all of this could start.

Any psychologist knows that the basic patterns of personality are established in the very early years. I know that it is sometimes possible for wonderful changes to take place in a person later in life. But for most of us, the type of persons we are was probably fairly well established before we went to school. This is why, important as the school, the church, the society as a whole are, they can generally only serve to reinforce or weaken or correct what is already there. They have their great role in shaping the thought and action of the adults who bring up the next generation of children.

It is almost certainly true that in earlier generations, in more stable societies, the family was spared many of the stresses and strains which it faces today. I am not, however, willing to romanticize or idealize some earlier forms of family life. We cannot reverse history, but even if we could, I suspect we would only be exchanging one set of problems for another. What we need to do is to look at the wonderful possibilities for family life which modern science, technology, psychology and education could make possible today and tomorrow.

MALE AND FEMALE

First we need a clear picture of what marriage and family life can be. Then perhaps slowly and falteringly, but at least with a sense of direction, we might be able to move toward a clear goal.

Certainly the intimate relationship of male and female is a part of God's scheme of things. And the gradual and persistent development of the idea of monogamous marriage seems to fit into this scheme. That the finest possibilities of the marriage relationship have often been thwarted by the attitudes of society and the church is, I believe, self-evident. When marriage is seen solely as a convenience for the procreation and care of children, with little concern for the growth and development of the husband and wife, much is lost. When wifehood was the only acceptable role for a woman (no matter to whom she was married) the best possibilities of the relationship could not be realized. When church and society have been unwilling to admit that tragic mistakes might be made, and refused any possibilities of repentance and forgiveness and a new start, marriage could be a mockery.

If we think of marriage, first of all, as a covenant made between a man and woman, similar in some mysterious way to the covenant God offers to each of his children, marriage can and should be a foretaste of heaven. Here two human beings—sinful, selfish, coming out of different families and perhaps very different backgrounds—enter into a relationship. It can be, and should be, the most important decision they ever make, for their whole future depends on it. How important it is, then, that they know as much about it as they can. But what do they know?

They both know something of marriage as a result of the homes in which they grew up. These may be good ideas, or very bad ones Because our society groups people so exclusively by ages, many young people have little opportunity to know and be with married couples other than their parents, to see some other possible patterns of relationships. An occasional church tries to meet this need by having married couples "sponsor" or advise youth groups, but we could use much more imagination along this line. Young people need a wider range of "images" of marriage.

Above all, however, they need help in understanding what it can mean to give oneself to another. If we could only find ways, in youth groups and in marriage instruction, to help people realize the deep, essential loneliness of every individual, and to see that one of the great gifts of marriage can be an alleviation of that loneliness! But it can only be this if there is real openness and communication. If, in marriage, we can find the one human being in the world before whom we can take off our mask, and not have to pretend any more, and still be sure of love and acceptance, we will be on the way to a really good relationship. If there is one person in the world who cares for me even when he knows all my faults and stupidities, I can move with a little more ease in every other relationship.

SEXUAL RELATIONSHIPS

No one will deny the importance of sexual relationship in marriage. But I suspect that every really happily married person would say that it is far less important than movies, books, advertising and even most courses in "preparation for marriage" make it out to be! Without downgrading sex, or upgrading it by making it mysterious and undiscussable, all of us who are concerned ought to be working on ways in which the deeper and more important aspects of marriage as a place for personal growth and maturing could be made clear, especially to the young.

I have a somewhat heretical notion here (and a recent article by Rollo May seems to be pointing to the same thing) that the rather startling sexual freedom of the present day may in some strange way actually lead to putting the physical sex aspect of marriage into a better perspective. This may allow the deep, interpersonal communion between two persons to be seen again as the heart of marriage.

Imagining back a few generations, it seems possible that in an era when most families lived and worked together on the farm or in the small family business, there was a certain underlying companionship in hard work; and sex was a physical fact accepted without much introspection or discussion. Children were an asset —more hands and feet for the family enterprise. Childlessness was considered the wife's fault and could be a serious burden for her to bear. When business moved out of the home, and women were more ornamental and a little less a necessity to the family livelihood, tensions began to build up in marriage. Women often felt "trapped" in a relationship with a man whom they hardly knew, and to whom they had less and less to say as the years passed. To many women, in the over-prudish era before World War I, sexual relationship was just one of the unpleasant prices a woman had to pay for the security of a home.

Then came the sex explosion of the twenties and thirties. Sex was the great new discovery. Everyone talked about it; it became the be-all and end-all of marriage. "Companionate marriage" was seriously proposed in the late twenties. Sex was so important that a couple had better try it out and see if they were sexually adjusted before entering into a permanent marriage. This isolation of the sexual relationship had little logic. Within a real relationship of trust and openness and mutual caring, sexual relations are a wonderful bond. Without the prior relationship sex is sheer physical release of tension.

I am inclined to think that today's youth, aided by the pill and antibiotics, so that the old fears of pregnancy and venereal disease are lessened, may at last be able to find more of the real meaning of marriage. Above all, it ought to be seen as a channel for human freedom and growth—a relationship between two people which is so creative and joyous that it is a parable of the relationship with God, and a setting within which children can grow up free and loving and uninhibited.

CHILDREN AND PARENTHOOD

Let us turn, then to parenthood. The desire for children seems to be built deep in human nature. Certainly when a man and a woman have a relationship which is wonderful and good, they find in the birth of children both a fulfillment and an opportunity. But, children also present the possibility of breaking the close bond between husband and wife. Here their inherited patterns of parent-child relationships can rear their ugly heads. What forms of discipline are right? How much acceptance and affection are right, without "spoiling" the children?

Surely this is a place where the church, if it were aware of the needs of its members, could make a great contribution. The simple fact needs to be known that in general there are two attitudes toward life and other people. Some people have a basically positive attitude. They assume that others are good, friendly, and mean well. They are open to new people and to new experiences. Their potential for growth is good. Others start life with a fearful, distrustful and negative attitude. They dare not be open or friendly lest they be rebuffed. Because of their own distrustful attitude, they elicit unfriendly responses, which confirms their worst suspicions. It is a wild over-generalization, but fundamentally true, that every human being falls into one of these categories.

And these patterns are developed in the home, in the earliest years. If parents could be helped to understand this, they could perhaps be helped not to inflict their own fears and uncertainties on their children. This would require, in our day, some frank discussion between parents about what they want for their children. Too often, these things are assumed and not discussed. Then tensions arise in regard to discipline, and the children, sensing disagreement between their parents, are either confused or, more often, learn to play one parent against the other.

If marriage for a man and woman can mean a relationship in which you are loved for what you are, rather than for what you accomplish, the family can begin to be the same kind of place for a child. Here he is loved just because he is himself. He may be disciplined when he breaks the rules, but he is still loved in the midst of discipline. The love of his parents is not conditional. It does not depend on his grades, or his achievements, or his social success. It is a human paradigm of God's love.

THEOLOGICAL REASSESSMENT

Is there any hope, in our high-pressured, status-seeking society, of re-educating people to the psychological and theological needs which the family could and should fulfill for its members? Many discussions of the role of the family stress its importance as the basic economic, or social, or educational unit of civilization. It is all of these, of course. But in church discussions of family life, there has been far too little emphasis, it seems to me, on the place of the family in the formation of Christian personality.

Indeed, for the modern Christian, the church itself has far too often become simply another instrument of society and culture. Martin Marty and others have written vividly of the way in which many modern American Christians see the church as the bulwark of the American way of life. It is seen as an instrument for undergirding our prevalent moral, economic and social standards and training people to conform to them.

What may be most needed, therefore, may be a theological re-assessment of the role of the family. Our work- and achievement-oriented society, which deeply influences family life and the rearing of children, denies the biblical and Protestant emphasis on justification by grace. Home, school and even the church put their stress on works. Parents teach children that they will be loved and approved if they are good, work hard, get good grades, outdo their fellows. Wives put pressure on their husbands to do well, get ahead, provide more and more. Husbands want their wives to conform to the standard of housekeeping and personal appearance promoted by advertising.

While it would be both unwise and unrealistic, in this interdependent era, to advocate the withdrawal of family life from society, making the home a refuge from the world, it might be possible for the emphasis on family life to be geared more consciously to the wholesome development of persons as we believe God wants them to be developed. Just as God has opened the mysteries of the physical universe to scientists, we can believe that he is allowing psychologists to discover his laws for the development of the human personality.

We need solid study on the theological implications of psychology and the psychological aspects of theology, if the church is really to be effective in helping with this area of human life. Psychology and human personality development should be much more carefully taught in our seminaries. Too much of the pastoral psychology now being taught is pathologically oriented, dealing with the "sick" rather than encouraging healthy growth. Churches, both national and local, could well have courses and seminars on this subject for clergy and laity.

Each new area of human knowledge which God opens to men carries with it the possibility of upsetting old ideas about religion and the church—and at the same time the possibility of moving ahead into forms which may be more constructive and closer to God's will.

12

The Bible and Sexuality

•

RICHARD ARMSTRONG

In the crisp straightforward style of a journalist Father Richard Armstrong, M.M. addresses himself to the issue of whether "anything goes" in sexual behavior. Director of The Christopher Movement, Fr. Armstrong has written dozens of issues of the popular *Christopher News Notes,* edited *Apostolic Renewal In The Seminary* and co-authored the annual publication, *Three Minutes A Day,* since 1961.

UNDER THE HEADING "Anything Goes—The Permissive Society," *Newsweek* magazine recently commented:

> Gradually and yet suddenly, a startling new atmosphere has arisen in which almost anything seems permissible in the arts, the media, the fashions and customs of our time. Writers openly use language that was banned only a short while ago; movies are nakeder and more outspoken than they have ever been, plays depict the most hidden human sexuality; provocation and display are the rule in dress; the most intimate subjects are openly and directly dealt with in schools, on television and in periodicals . . .

The prevailing climate of permissiveness is causing much public confusion about the right and wrong use of sexuality.

The following highlights from the Bible on the subject may serve as a stimulus to your own prayerful reading, straight thinking and constructive action.

". . . IN THE IMAGE OF GOD . . ."

"God created man in the image of Himself, in the image of God He created him, male and female He created them." (Genesis 1:27)

An image can mean a lot of things. Look in the mirror and what do you see—an image of yourself. "A chip off the old block . . ." "The picture of his father . . ." Images are like the real thing. So much so that they sometimes startle us.

They are also very different. Man, unlike God—yet like him. Man can think. Man can love. The human person, who thinks and loves. God, who is all knowledge and love. Unequal partners, one imaging the Other.

Anything of lasting value in our hectic world affirms this basic dignity of the human person: by promoting his best interests—physical, mental, spiritual; by helping him grow in knowledge and responsibility; by honoring—never violating—the total personality of another human being. Like all other forms of communication between people, sound sexual relationships are built on mutual respect. You—and everyone else for that matter—are made in the image of God. It's worth thinking about.

". . . MALE AND FEMALE HE CREATED THEM . . ."

When God made them male and female he told us something about himself. God is a Lover—strong and steady—Who never deserts his beloved. (Hosea 14:5)

God is far more attentive to his people than a mother to the baby at her breast. (Isaiah 49:15)

And he told us something about people: He designed physical differences. He gave special needs. He granted definite privileges.

Over and above the physical distinctions, God invests human beings with masculine or feminine potentialities. This sexuality is a characteristic of each one's total personality. It grows, develops and reveals itself through childhood, youth and adulthood.

Sexuality reaches a new and joyous stage when two persons, freely and knowingly, pledge themselves forever to union of mind, heart and body. This we call marriage. If marriage is forever and its gift is total here begin to emerge the mysterious workings of a divine plan. Through the mystery of human sexuality God offers men and women opportunities for personal enrichment that point beyond self to the co-creation of new life.

NEED FOR PERSPECTIVE

"If you wish to enter into life, keep the commandments." (Matthew 19:17)

A wealthy young man approached Jesus with the question: "Master, what good deed must I do to possess eternal life?" The eager questioner was apparently looking for something extraordinary. The Lord's answer must have come as a letdown. Far from giving out any magic formula, he restated several of the commandments relating to love of neighbor: "You must not kill. You must not commit adultery. You must not bring false witness. Honor your father and mother, and you must love your neighbor as yourself." (Matthew 19:18)

The Gospel story goes on to make a further point. But what concerns us here is that Jesus presents sexual morality as only one among the many requirements for entering into life. He neither exaggerates its importance, nor minimizes it. And neither should we.

CALL TO SERVICE

"My brothers, you were called, as you know, to liberty; but be careful, or this liberty will provide an opening for self-indulgence. Serve one another, rather, in works of love." (Galatians 5:13)

Freedom is the launching pad for human activity. It exists for service to others, not self-indulgence.

To serve another person in love can mean many things. Engaged couples do so when they strive to communicate with each other honestly and in depth on significant matters: ideals, religion, parenthood, life goals, finances.

They work together to produce a oneness of purpose before marriage so that their coming together in one flesh may communicate the best that each has to offer.

Love expressed through service, made supple by affection and firm discipline, is far more likely to support two maturing persons for life, nourish their children and provide a hopeful example to the world around them. Freedom is God's gift and man's challenge.

DODGING THE ISSUE

"Some days later Felix came with his wife Drusilla who was a Jewess. He sent for Paul and gave him a hearing on the subject of faith in Christ Jesus. But when he began to treat of righteousness, self-control and the coming Judgment, Felix took fright and said, 'You may go for the present; I will send for you when I find it convenient.'" (Acts 24:24,25)

The Roman governor Felix. A complex man. Living in a ruthlessly competitive world. Something within him was caught by the message and personality of the prisoner Paul. But it was so hard, he was not above taking a bribe. "Righteousness" sent a chill through him. He had seduced Drusilla away from her husband. "Self-control" was a touchy subject. The Apostle Paul put it on the line. Faith in Jesus: No shady deals. No stealing other people's wives. Personal accountability at the judgment seat of God. Christianity—then and now—leaves no room to pick and choose. Felix dodged the issue. What about us?

Not Alone

"You can trust God not to let you be tried beyond your strength, and with any trial he will give you a way out of it and the strength to bear it." (1 Corinthians 10:13)

Everybody is tempted. And the odd thing is, nearly everybody feels alone when it happens. Alone. And powerless. Nothing could be further from the truth. God is faithful, so we're not alone. He doesn't allow us to get in over our heads. We can draw on his strength to find a way out.

The peculiar attractiveness of sexual temptation can throw us for a loss. Despite the remorse that is likely to follow, it seems as if too much is being asked of us to say "no."

Other people have worked through the severest trials against fidelity and the right use of their sexuality. Some are doing so right now. God is with them—and he wills to be with us. If we let him.

Fresh Start

" 'Woman, where are they? Has no one condemned you?' 'No one, sir,' she replied. 'Neither do I condemn you,' said Jesus, 'go away, and don't sin any more.' " (John 8:10,11)

A woman caught in the act of adultery. Her accusers brought her to Jesus for judgment. The punishment in the Law was death by stoning. But Jesus came to bring life, not death. Death to sin, yes. But new life in God. He could see that she was sorry—more sorry than words could express. The Lord's compassion gently led her toward the authentic love she had mistakenly sought in the shadows.

Jesus was not shocked by sin. He neither explained it away nor did he harp on it. He did what was better yet. He forgave it. And, when confronted by sorrow that accepts the hardships of a fresh start, he still does.

ACCENTS OF LOVE

"How beautiful you are, my love, how beautiful you are! Your eyes, behind your veil are doves . . . Your lips are a scarlet thread and your words enchanting . . . You are wholly beautiful, my love, and without a blemish." (Song of Songs 4:1,3,7)

In this biblical text, a young man praises his bride-to-be in tender human terms. The sentiments he expresses are old and ever new. They have been echoed and re-echoed in song, sonnets and plain-spoken words throughout the ages.

As long as men and women search for ways to say "I love you," the Song of Songs will be a stirring reminder that the sexuality granted to human beings is good. It is from God himself.

We have it on divine authority that sexuality finds its fulfill-ment in marriage—the joyous intensity of which foreshadows our eternal oneness with him and one another.

The entire Bible is a story of God's love for mankind. It speaks in accents that call forth a response of personal faith, of undying hope and of a love that goes beyond platitudes to a very practical service to others.

PROMISE OF FOREVER

"Marriage is to be honored by all, and marriages are to be kept undefiled." (Hebrews 13:4)

Husbands and wives tune in on a meaning that has already been set by God. It can be played with a million individual variations. But the meaning does not change: "I give myself to you, not just for this minute or this hour—not just in this act, but in all that I do—forever." It is a promise of enduring love. Respect for both persons, made in God's image requires it. The care and upbringing of children demands it. The social structure of the community and nation rests upon it. Marriage is to be held in honor by all because the welfare of all is affected by it.

SPLIT-LEVEL MORALITY

"People of immoral lives, idolaters, adulterers, catamites, sodomites, thieves, usurers, drunkards, slanderers and swindlers will never inherit the Kingdom of God. These are the sort of people some of you were once, but now you have been washed clean, and sanctified, and justified through the name of the Lord Jesus Christ and through the Spirit of our God." (1 Corinthians 6:9-11)

Among the Christian community at Corinth, a troublesome few totally misunderstood the message of the Apostle Paul. They drove a sharp wedge between body and spirit. To them, "anything goes" in matters of the body; you could still be "spiritual." A split-level morality.

The Kingdom of God can be seen in personal worship of the Father, not idolatry . . . in the joyful embrace of married men and women, not in fornication or perversion . . . in generosity, not avarice or theft . . . in self-mastery, not drunkenness.

Paul minced no words. The Kingdom of God is not so much where you are as what you are. It is the power of Christ already at work within you.

THE CHOICE IS YOURS

In the midst of a "permissive society" of their own, the early Christians were confronted by St. Paul with a basic decision; give way to self-indulgence or follow the Spirit of God. The consequences of each were plain to see—and still are: "If you are guided by the Spirit you will be in no danger of yielding to self-indulgence, since self-indulgence is the opposite of the Spirit, the Spirit is totally against such a thing, and it is precisely because the two are so opposed that you do not always carry out your good intentions.

"If you are led by the Spirit, no law can touch you. When self-indulgence is at work the results are obvious: fornication, gross indecency and sexual irresponsibility; idolatry and sorcery; feuds and wrangling, jealousy, bad temper and quarrels; disagreements, factions, envy; drunkenness, orgies and similar things . . .

"What the Spirit brings is very different: love, joy, peace, patience, kindness, goodness, trustfulness, gentleness and self-control." (Galatians 5:16-24)

All biblical quotations in this chapter are from the Jerusalem Bible.

13

Study Helps

•

I. INTERFAITH STATEMENT ON SEX EDUCATION
   by The National Council of Churches' Commission
   on Marriage and the Family
   The Synagogue Council of America's Committee on Family
   and
   The United States Catholic Conference Family Life Bureau

A WORD ABOUT THIS STATEMENT

This statement was drafted by the Interfaith Commission on Marriage and Family Life created by the three sponsoring organizations.

This statement develops further some of the affirmations made in the Commission's earlier Joint Statement on Marriage and Family Life in the United States (see part II).

It is offered to our respective communions to stimulate their activities within their own groups and to guide their support of the increasing number of community efforts in sex education.

It is offered to community leaders and teachers as a statement of the common affirmations of the major faith groups of our country.

The Interfaith Commission welcomes reports of significant interfaith projects or involvement in community and school activities.

I

Human sexuality is a gift of God, to be accepted with thanksgiving and used with reverence and joy. It is more than a mechanical instinct. Its many dimensions are intertwined with the total personality and character of the individual. Sex is a dynamic urge or power, arising from one's basic maleness or femaleness, and having complex physical, psychological and social dimensions. These dimensions, we affirm, must be shaped and guided by spiritual and moral considerations which derive from our Judeo-Christian heritage. The heritage teaches us that the source of values to guide human behavior is in God.

The sexual attitudes of children develop as part of their general social attitudes. Furthermore, respectful and considerate sexual attitudes help create healthy social attitudes. When the family and society view sex as loving and fulfilling, rather than prurient and exploitative, then both the social and sexual attitudes of children benefit. A healthful approach to sexual relations, willingness and ability to impart sexual information in a manner proportionate to the child's stage of development—these are among the elements which foster healthy sexual attitudes and behavior in the young. So, also, is resistance to social pressures which in some instances lead to premature sophistication or unhealthy attitudes in young people.

Responsibility for sex education belongs primarily to the child's parents or guardians. A home permeated by justice and love is the seedbed of sound sexual development among all family members. Both the attitudes and the activities of the parents—toward each other and toward each child as an individual—affect this development. Healthy attitudes toward sex begin in the child's earliest years; they can best develop in an atmosphere that fosters in him a deep sense of his own self-worth, bolstered by love and understanding.

Sex education is not, however, only for the young; it is a lifelong task whose aim is to help individuals develop their sexuality in a manner suited to their stage of life.

We recognize that some parents desire supplementary assistance from church or synagogue and from other agencies. Each community of faith should provide resources, leadership and opportunities as appropriate for its young people to learn about their development into manhood and womanhood, and for adults to grow in understanding of their roles as men and women in family and society in the light of their religious heritage.

In addition to parents and the religious community, the school and other community agencies can have a vital role in sex education in two particular ways:

1. They can integrate sound sexual information and attitudes with the total education which the child receives in social studies, civics, literature, history, home economics and the biological and behavioral sciences.

2. They can reach the large numbers of young people whose families have no religious identification but who need to understand their own sexuality and their role in society.

For those who would introduce sex education into the schools, however, the question of values and norms for sexual behavior is a problem—indeed, the most difficult problem. It is important that sex education not be reduced to the mere commmunication of information. Rather, this significant area of experience should be placed in a setting where rich human, personal and spiritual values can illuminate it and give it meaning. In such a setting, we are convinced it is not only possible but necessary to recognize certain basic moral principles, not as sectarian religious doctrine but as the moral heritage of Western civilization.

The challenge of resolving this problem of values in a pluralistic society makes it all the more imperative that communities planning to introduce sex education into the schools not only call upon educators to become involved in decisions about goals and techniques, but also invite parents and professionals in the community to take part in shaping such a curriculum.

To those groups responsible for development of school and community programs in sex education we suggest the following guidelines:

a) Such education should strive to create understanding and conviction that decisions about sexual behavior must be based on moral and ethical values, as well as on considerations of physical and emotional health, fear, pleasure, practical consequences, or concepts of personality development.

b) Such education must respect the cultural, familial and religious backgrounds and beliefs of individuals and must teach that the sexual development and behavior of each individual cannot take place in a vacuum but are instead related to the other aspects of his life and to his moral, ethical and religious codes.

c) It should point out how sex is distorted and exploited in our society and how this places heavy responsibility upon the individual, the family and institutions to cope in a constructive manner with the problem thus created.

d) It must recognize that in school sex education, insofar as it relates to moral and religious beliefs and values, complements the education conveyed through the family, the church or the synagogue. Sex education in the schools must proceed constructively, with understanding, tolerance and acceptance of difference.

e) It must stress the many points of harmony between moral

values and beliefs about what is right and wrong that are held in common by the major religions on the one hand and generally accepted legal, social, psychological, medical and other values held in common by service professions and society generally.

f) Where strong differences of opinion exist on what is right and wrong sexual behavior, objective, informed and dignified discussion of both sides of such questions should be encouraged. However, in such cases, neither the sponsors of an educational program nor the teachers should attempt to give definite answers or to represent their personal moral and religious beliefs as the consensus of the major religions or of society generally.

g) Throughout such education human values and human dignity must be stressed as major bases for decisions of right and wrong; attitudes that build such respect should be encouraged as right, and those that tear down such respect should be condemned as wrong.

h) Such education should teach that sexuality is a part of the whole person and an aspect of his dignity as a human being.

i) It should teach that people who love each other try not to do anything that will harm each other.

j) It should teach that sexual intercourse within marriage offers the greatest possibility for personal fulfillment and social growth.

k) Finally, such a program of education must be based on sound content and must employ sound methods; it must be conducted by teachers and leaders qualified to do so by training and temperament.

The increased concern and interest in this vital area of human experience now manifested by parents, educators and religious leaders are cause for gratitude. We urge all to take a more active role—each in his own area of responsibility and competence—in promoting sound leadership and programs in sex education. We believe it possible to help our sons and daughters achieve a richer, fuller understanding of their sexuality, so that their children will enter a world where men and women live and work together in understanding, co-operation and love.

II. A JOINT STATEMENT ON MARRIAGE AND
FAMILY LIFE IN THE UNITED STATES

Keenly aware of the role religion ascribes to the home and family life and keenly aware of the powerful and pervasive social conditions which threaten to undermine human dignity, marriage and family life in America, we, as representatives of the major religions —Catholic, Jewish, Orthodox, and Protestant—wish to bring the religious teachings of our respective faiths to bear upon our society and to join with all men of good will to create a healthier social climate in which family life in America can flourish and be strong.

There are large areas of agreement and numerous possibilities for joint programs and action, although we recognize and respect the differences of approach, emphases and contributions of each major faith.

To help families develop foundations for personally meaningful and socially responsible behavior, we offer the following affirmations on which our historic faiths unite.

We believe and unite in affirming, that God, the Creator of the Universe and the Father of all mankind, did create us male and female and did establish families as part of his Divine Plan. Because of our understanding of this plan, we believe and unite in affirming that our sexuality is a wondrous gift from God to be accepted with thanksgiving and used within marriage and with reverence and joy.

We believe and unite in affirming that our understanding of God's plan for marriage ideally calls for lifelong commitment in fidelity to a continuing, supportive relationship in which each partner helps the other to develop to fullest capacity. We are united in our belief that God is an active partner in sustaining and enriching the husband-wife relationship in marriage.

We believe and unite in affirming that children are a trust from God and that parenthood is a joyous, though strenuous, adventure in partnership with God for the procreation and nurturing of each child. Parenthood calls for the responsible use of all of our God-given talents and abilities in this adventure.

We believe and unite in affirming that family life is the cradle of personality and character for each child and creates an environment for the societal values of each succeeding generation as well as the principal source of meaningful personal relations for each adult member of our society. All children need a father and a mother firmly united in love to guide their growth into manhood or womanhood and to provide the emotional security that fosters development toward mature and responsible relationships between men and women.

We believe that the family is the cornerstone of our society. It shapes the attitudes, the hopes, the ambitions, the values of every citizen. The child is usually damaged when family living collapses. When this happens on a massive scale, the community itself is crippled.

There are no easy answers to all the complex problems facing marriage and family living in the world today, and we are aware that there are many fronts on which we must work. We can never finish the task; neither are we free to ignore it.

Therefore, we the major religious groups in the U.S., join forces in exploring all ways and means available to preserve and strengthen family life in America to the end that each person may enjoy fulfillment in dignity, justice, and peace.

III. A GUIDE FOR GROUP STUDY AND DISCUSSION

Prepared by William H. Genné

In his guidance to study groups, the Rev. William H. Genné re-emphasizes some principles he wrote into the volume of *Sex, Family and Society In Theological Focus*. His insistence upon openness, integrity and adequate time will impress groups as realistic for the goal of learning. Mr. Genné is co-ordinator of the Commission on Marriage and Family, National Council of Churches of Christ in the U.S.A. His previous writings include *Husbands and Pregnancy;*

and with co-author Elizabeth S. Genné he has written *Christians and the Crisis in Sex Morality* and edited *Foundations for Christian Family Policy.*

Any group of concerned persons may use this book as the basis for a series of study and discussion meetings. Whether or not they meet under church auspices is unimportant so long as they are interested in exploring the relevance of the Christian faith to contemporary men and women.

The group may be composed of men or of women or of both together. They may be drawn from a neighborhood, a congregation, a community organization, a campus, a group that works together, or any combination of persons. They may meet in any setting: home, classroom, clubroom, church.

There are certain conditions, however, which must be met if this venture is to prove worth while. The conditions are these:

1. Time: Each person must be willing to commit the time necessary for a thoughtful reading of the book and for responsible participation in the group. It takes time for any assemblage of persons to become a group who really hear each other and understand and trust each other.

This guide is designed for a minimum of three sessions. Each topic might be expanded to two or three sessions, and so the series might continue for eight or twelve weeks. Any number of sessions between four and twelve that suits the group is recommended.

2. Openness: The quality of openness has two aspects:

(a) Openness to the outside—to new truth and the power of the Holy Spirit. The writers of this book have wrestled with many difficult and dismaying questions. They remind us of features about life and ourselves we would rather forget. They have in some instances put our unspoken doubts and perplexities into words. There are points where they challenge us to new insights into the meaning and power of the gospel. We must be willing to open ourselves to these probings and also to the working of the Holy Spirit within us.

(b) Openness from the inside. If our group is to be real, mean-

Study Helps

ingful, and helpful we must be willing to give; to expose our own doubts and anxieties and to share our resources. We must grow in the honesty and openness with which we can participate in the group.

3. Integrity: The openness we have just mentioned is not the openness of a sieve that cannot hold anything. Rather, it is the openness of a hand that must open its clenched fist before it can grasp something new. Therefore, each member of the group must reaffirm his integrity as a person and as a child of God. We must be willing to cast off the masks we wear to protect ourselves and to impress others. We must admit how each of us has been scared and scarred by the way we have been reared in our contemporary culture. At the same time we must mobilize those resources of health and sanity which can help to make us whole.

Of course sex is an emotionally charged subject. The very intensity of some of the more pathological expressions we see all about us is a testimony of its power just as its indescribable beauty and ecstasy can ennoble a man or woman and help to create a noble culture.

Unless you are ready to meet these conditions of time, openness, and integrity it will be better not to begin. If, however, you are willing to dare to make an honest effort, let us see what lies ahead.

The topics listed for each session are inextricably intertwined. Each draws on material from several chapters of the book. It is suggested that each member read the whole book before beginning the discussions in order that each will be free to draw on the whole range of thought.

This guide is not keyed to a chapter-by-chapter progress through the book, but rather to three basic foci for questions and discussion. The group leader should create an atmosphere of freedom to draw on the insights of the total book in any one session. The questions here are meant to be thought primers. The members of your group will think of many more of equal importance to them. Not all the questions which follow need to be used.

The important thing is to dig, to explore, to grow in our understanding of the gospel as it empowers each of us to attain the full stature of the manhood or womanhood with which God has endowed us.

SESSION I—CONTEMPORARY SEXUAL BEHAVIOR AND THE CHURCH

(Refer to Chapters 1, 2, 3, 4 and 10)

In the first session, the group could begin with a collective book review, starting with Harvey Cox's conviction that we face a new phase of responsibility about sexual behavior.

Dr. Cox writes of four C's: competence, compensation, communication and compulsion. Review what these mean to the writer. Then allow the study group to face such questions as: Do these four C's present any threat to Christian freedom? What danger is there that our own discussion in the church will reflect a previous stage of discussion outside the church and therefore have only marginal reference to frontier points of the secular situation? Do younger adults better understand the Cox chapter than over-forty members of the group? Or is there any age difference regarding sex attitudes? Do older married persons remember their sexual frustrations and sexual decisions they faced in youth?

Dr. Winter in Chapter 3 says that Christian ethics are shaped in the church's pastoral ministry. What, if anything, does this mean to you? He refers also to "the recovery of the body," an odd term. In what ways has the body been lost in contemporary society?

How can our education about sexuality be made relevant to the various subcultural groups in community life? The influence of social and economic conditions on family instability, prostitution and other "pathologies" is well established. How do our ethical choices in these matters relate to our sexual ethics?

According to Dr. Lehmann, in what ways is sexuality fundamental to human fulfillment? How is belonging with someone else both a mystery and a threat? What does the identity-freedom-fidelity syndrome signify about sex differentiation and connection?

Dr. Kirkendall writes from outside the church's theological commitments in his humanistic approach. Does this make any difference to his writings about sex—or to your understanding of his material? How does the group react to his ten "non-statistical" observations on our contemporary scene? What is your response to this author's distinction between Christian sources and humanist sources of authority for moral decision?

Kinsey's now famous statistics are reviewed in Dr. Wynn's opening chapter. So is the literature studied by The World Council of Churches assembly at Uppsala in 1968 (Excerpt: "sleeping together may become as ordinary as eating together"). Do such statements any longer have the power to shake the reader? Or has what Dr. Cox calls "a broader, deeper and more candid conversation among Christians about sexuality" prepared us for these?

Theologians, Dr. Wynn insists, are not only confounded by such sexual data; but they aren't really the detached scholars we had supposed. Is his picture of the theologian working under pressure to catch up to life's challenges fair? Is his clue that the Christian tradition nevertheless offers guidelines (e.g. avoidance of repeating the past, of all things) realistic?

Do readers find elsewhere in the book indications of the new morality discussed in Chapter 1? Where? And how is it presented? Make some judicious comparisons of these authors and their views.

SESSION II—THE CHRISTIAN TRADITION

(*Refer to Chapters 6, 7, 8 and the Appendix* Interfaith Statement)

Contrasting the contemporary situation, its Kinsey era statistics and new morality in Session I with the Christian tradition reflected in these chapters presents an exercise in history. We have roots in the past; and we remain a part of our tradition even when modern events have altered our mores and our outlook.

If the leadership available to the group makes possible a lecture-and-discussion approach, the material in these chapters is especially adaptable to that method. The lecture should be organized into brief units with ready, frequent discussion rather than into one full statement followed by a fatigued period of questions and comments.

Questions that arise from these chapters include, among numerous others that will occur to the reader, the following examples.

Dr. Piper has some rather sharp challenges for some of the modern approaches to sex ethics. How do you react to his criticisms? Does the biblical view of man "speak to your condition"? Does it hold any additional fulfillment for you? How does Dr. Piper's discussion of "Sex and Creation" enlarge our understanding of the role of sex in the cosmos?

Man's sexuality can be best understood, according to Dr. Piper, in the light of the destiny God has given man. What does this mean to you?

How does Dr. Piper's position relate to Father Thomas' position when the latter talks of "the relevant dimensions" and says, "The quality of being 'sexed' has profound implications for both man and society"? What additional implications do you see?

Fr. Thomas, after tracing the development of Roman Catholic sex ethics, cites some of the growing edges of challenge between Catholic scholars and theologians. Can you discern similar movements among other religious groups, either Christian or Jewish?

Dr. Bailey (Ch. 8) tells that St. Paul was probably temperamentally averse to marriage. How did this affect the Apostle's philosophy of sexual relations? But in what ways was he also strangely modern in his writings?

And where, according to Dr. Bailey, did the Christian tradition derive its negative strain of thought about sex? How can we interpret his conviction that "the Christian tradition was a living and growing thing, . . . bearing witness to the new spirit which Christianity gradually infused into marriage and sexual relationships"?

If he is correct in the concluding paragraph of Chapter 8 that our sexual ethic is being currently remolded, how can its new form make the will of God more clearly known? That would seem to comprise a very difficult task in the face of current circumstances that seem to obscure the will of God.

The Interfaith Statement on Sex Education to be found in the Appendix is brief enough for the group to read silently while in session. From this experience of guided reading, they can build an entire evening's discussion on the topic of sex education. The point-by-point consideration of sub-paragraphs *a* through *k* will organize a useful method for thinking through the issues of sex education, which has become a controversial program in some communities.

SESSION III—DIVERGENT VIEWS OF THE CHURCH'S RESPONSIBILITY

(Refer to Chapters 5, 9, 11 and 12)

The sub-title of the book, *Divergent Views*, is reflected throughout its entirety, yet in special ways within these chapters. Canon Dunstan writes that reasonable men do not suppose that what can be technically accomplished is desirable to accomplish. And in that context he discusses the contraceptive pill. What has the canon to say about the papal encyclical, *Humanae Vitae*? How does he believe the encyclical subordinates "the characteristically human to the characteristically animal"? What does man's "lordship over the organic world" mean in sexual relationship? How does he define man's limits in human sexual love? Does the discussion of death shed new information for us in relation to life and its sexual processes?

In Chapter 11 Dr. Wedel emphasizes the freedom required by true love—both between man and God and man and woman. What threats does this freedom pose to us as persons and to our social structures?

Dr. Wedel comments that our work and achievement-oriented families deny our biblical and Protestant faith. What changes would be necessary to bring our family life into harmony with our faith?

To the theological agenda of Dr. Cox, Dr. Bonthius would add two more C's—consequences and celebration. What are the theological implications of these?

What elements of traditional ethical approaches still appeal to us? How do the newer ethical approaches appeal to us—and frighten us?

The *Interfaith Statement* pleads for a total community effort of home, church and school for sexual enlightenment. What opportunities and obligations do we have in this regard as citizens?

As concerned persons, how can we create "cells of wholeness and health" regarding sexual matters in our churches?

What next steps does our group wish to take to continue the study-action encounter in our community?—in our church?—in our homes?—in our personal lives?

Index*

* Prepared by Calvin Steck